THE LIBRARY OF
AMERICAN
LIVES AND TIMES™

PHILLIS WHEATLEY

A Revolutionary Poet

Jacquelyn McLendon

The Rosen Publishing Group's
PowerPlus Books™
New York

For my family:
Keanna, Nancy, Lamarr, Carl, and Ernie
and in memory of
Gertrude and Ernest O. McLendon Sr.
and Ernest O. McLendon III

Published in 2003 by The Rosen Publishing Group, Inc.
29 East 21st Street, New York, NY 10010

Editor's Note: All quotations have been reproduced as they appeared in the letters and diaries from which they were borrowed. No correction was made to the inconsistent spelling that was common in that time period.

First Edition

Library of Congress Cataloging-in-Publication Data

McLendon, Jacquelyn Y.
Phillis Wheatley : a revolutionary poet / Jacquelyn McLendon.
  p. cm. — (The library of American lives and times)
Summary: A biography of the former slave, Phillis Wheatley, who became known as a poet and social commentator.
Includes bibliographical references (p.) and index.
ISBN 0-8239-5750-0 (library binding)
1. Wheatley, Phillis, 1753–1784—Juvenile literature. 2. Poets, American—18th century—Biography—Juvenile literature. 3. African American women poets—Biography—Juvenile literature. 4. Slaves—United States—Biography—Juvenile literature. 5. African American poets—Biography—Juvenile literature. [1. Wheatley, Phillis, 1753–1784. 2. Poets, American. 3. Slaves. 4. African Americans—Biography. 5. Women—Biography.] I. Title. II. Series.
PS866.W5 Z66 2003
811'.1—dc21

2001007875

AEM-3360

CONTENTS

1. Birth of a Poet

Phillis Wheatley was an African American poet who lived during the eighteenth century. She was only fourteen years old when her first poem, "On Messrs. Hussey and Coffin," was published in the Rhode Island newspaper *Newport Mercury* in 1767. A poem that became one of her most famous, "On the Death of the Rev. Mr. George Whitefield. 1770," was published when she was just seventeen, and she then began to earn a reputation as a poet. In 1773, she became the first African American to publish a book of poetry. Her book *Poems on Various Subjects, Religious and Moral* contained thirty-nine of Phillis Wheatley's poems and was published in London, England, through the patronage of Selina Hastings, the countess of Huntingdon.

Writing a book of poems was an especially great accomplishment for Phillis, not only because she was so

Opposite: This eighteenth-century portrait of Phillis Wheatley is believed to have been made by Scipio Moorhead, an African American slave. Wheatley was America's first well known black author. Her writings helped to challenge people's assumptions about African inferiority.

An ELEGIAC
POEM,

On the DEATH of that celebrated Divine, and eminent Servant of JESUS CHRIST, the late Reverend, and pious

GEORGE WHITEFIELD,

Chaplain to the Right Honourable the Countess of HUNTINGDON, &c. &c.

Who made his Exit from this transitory State, to dwell in the celestial Realms of

Bliss, on LORD's-Day, 30th of September, 1770, when he was seiz'd with a Fit of the Asthma, at NEWBURY-PORT, near BOSTON, in NEW-ENGLAND. In which is a Condolatory Address to His truly noble Benefactress the worthy and pious Lady HUNTINGDON,---and the Orphan-Children in GEORGIA ; who, with many Thousands, are left, by the Death of this great Man, to lament the Loss of a Father, Friend, and Benefactor.

By PHILLIS, a Servant Girl of 17 Years of Age, belonging to Mr. J. WHEATLEY, of BOSTON :---And has been but 9 Years in this Country from Africa.

HAIL happy Saint on thy immortal throne !
　To thee complaints of grievance are unknown ;
We hear no more the music of thy tongue,
Thy wonted auditories cease to throng.
Thy lessons in unequal'd accents flow'd !
While emulation in each bosom glow'd ;
Thou didst, in strains of eloquence refin'd,
Inflame the soul, and captivate the mind.
Unhappy we, the setting Sun deplore !
Which once was splendid, but it shines no more ;
He leaves this earth for Heaven's unmeasur'd height :
And worlds unknown, receive him from our sight ;
There WHITEFIELD wings, with rapid course his way,
And sails to Zion, through vast seas of day.

　When his AMERICANS were burden'd sore,
When streets were crimson'd with their guiltless gore !
Unrival'd friendship in his breast now strove :
The fruit thereof was charity and love
Towards America-----couldst thou do more
Than leave thy native home, the British shore,
To cross the great Atlantic's wat'ry road,
To see America's distress'd abode ?
Thy prayers, great Saint, and thy incessant cries,
Have pierc'd the bosom of thy native skies !
Thou moon hast seen, and ye bright stars of light
Have witness been of his requests by night !
He pray'd that grace in every heart might dwell :
He long'd to see America excell ;
He charg'd its youth to let the grace divine
Arise, and in their future actions shine ;
He offer'd THAT he did himself receive,

A greater gift not GOD himself can give :
He urg'd the need of HIM to every one ;
It was no less than GOD's co-equal SON !
Take HIM ye wretched for your only good ;
Take HIM ye starving souls to be your food.
Ye thirsty, come to this life giving stream :
Ye Preachers, take him for your joyful theme :
Take HIM, " my dear AMERICANS," he said,
Be your complaints in his kind bosom laid :
Take HIM ye Africans, he longs for you ;
Impartial SAVIOUR, is his title due :
If you will chuse to walk in grace's road,
You shall be sons, and kings, and priests to GOD.

　Great COUNTESS ! we Americans revere
Thy name, and thus condole thy grief sincere :
We mourn with thee, that TOMB obscurely plac'd,
In which thy Chaplain undisturb'd doth rest.
New-England sure, doth feel the ORPHAN's smart ;
Reveals the true sensations of his heart :
Since this fair Sun, withdraws his golden rays,
No more to brighten these distressful days !
His lonely Tabernacle, sees no more
A WHITEFIELD landing on the British shore :
Then let us view him in yon azure skies :
Let every mind with this lov'd object rise.
No more can he exert his lab'ring breath,
Seiz'd by the cruel messenger of death.
What can his dear AMERICA return ?
But drop a tear upon his happy urn,
Thou tomb, shalt safe retain thy sacred trust,
Till life divine re-animate his dust.

Sold by EZEKIEL RUSSELL, in Queen-Street, and JOHN BOYLES, in Marlboro'-Street.

young, but also because she was a slave. She had been brought from Africa to America in 1761, when she was estimated to be about seven or eight years old. She was sold at a slave market to the Wheatley family in Boston, Massachusetts. As was customary, she was given their last name. Her first name was taken from the slave ship *Phillis*, on which she had arrived in Boston. The Wheatleys purchased her for the purpose of doing household chores and being a personal attendant, or helper, for Mrs. Susannah Wheatley. However, Phillis proved to be especially frail and was not suited for strenuous, physical work. Because of Phillis's obvious intelligence, the Wheatleys decided to educate her.

Many facts of Phillis Wheatley's early life are unknown, but she was probably kidnapped from her home, which is believed to have been in the Senegambia region of western Africa. During the Atlantic slave trade, which began in the early fifteenth century, kidnapping Africans from their villages was one of the ways in which the European traders obtained slaves. The kidnapping of Africans was often done by other Africans in exchange for goods that the European traders offered to them. Ottobah Cugoano, an African writing in 1787 about his slave experiences said, "I was first kidnapped and betrayed by my

---

Opposite: Wheatley's poem on the death of the well-known preacher George Whitefield in 1770 made her famous in Boston. Although Whitefield did own slaves, he was known to speak out against their ill treatment. He also supported the education of some blacks.

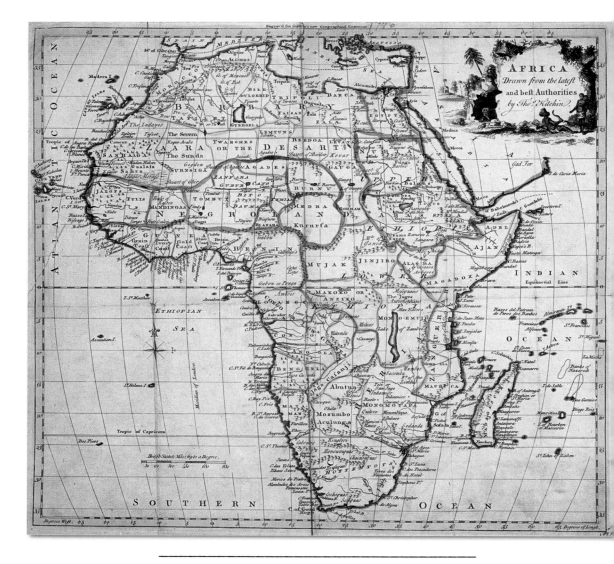

Like hundreds of thousands of other Africans of her time,
Phillis Wheatley was captured by slave traders in Africa
and was brought by ship to America to be sold at auction.
Thomas Kitchin made this map of Africa in 1776.

This hand-colored woodcut, created around 1790, shows captured Africans on a forced march to the port or the market to be sold as slaves. They would be auctioned off to bidders who would make them perform difficult labor and who would deprive them of their basic rights.

own complexion. . . . but if there were no buyers, there would be no sellers." These "buyers," or traders, also obtained slaves by trading goods with some chiefs of the African villages in exchange for their prisoners of war.

The captured Africans were marched to the coast on foot and were sold to African middlemen, who traded them to Europeans. The journey from inland, where the Africans were obtained, to the coast usually took weeks, and the captured Africans might be sold many times before reaching the coast. They were then imprisoned in

This engraving of a slave castle was created by Theodor de Bry between 1561 and 1623. Slave castles were large buildings with dungeons, where Africans were imprisoned before being shipped off into slavery. Africans were often beaten and killed in these dungeons.

slave castles or forts along the African coast before being loaded onto ships that would take them across the Atlantic Ocean to the West Indies, to South America, and to North America. The voyage from Africa across the Atlantic Ocean came to be known as the Middle Passage.

The Middle Passage was a horrible experience for the captured Africans, not just because they were being taken far away from their homeland, but also because they were horribly mistreated on the voyage. African men, women, and children were crammed aboard ships where the space had been divided into several decks to carry as many captives as possible. These decks were typically only about 3 feet (1 m) high, making it impossible for people to stand up. Therefore, the captives had to lie down day and night, with their hands and feet chained. It was so crowded that there was usually no space between one person and the next.

The Africans were poorly fed, and the water they were given to drink was foul. Conditions were so filthy that many people caught diseases and died. In addition, the crews aboard these ships were known to abuse the slaves. They beat them for no reason, and the women

During the Middle Passage to America, African slaves
sometimes were thrown overboard to drown in the ocean.
There were also slaves who chose to jump overboard,
preferring death to the life of slavery lying ahead.

Death of Capt. Ferrer, the Captain of the Amistad, July, 1839.

Don Jose Ruiz and Don Pedro Montez, of the Island of Cuba, having purchased fifty-three slaves at Havana, recently imported from Africa, put them on board the Amistad, Capt. Ferrer, in order to transport them to Principe, another port on the Island of Cuba. After being out from Havana about four days, the African captives on board, in order to obtain their freedom, and return to Africa, armed themselves with cane knives, and rose upon the Captain and crew of the vessel. Capt. Ferrer and the cook of the vessel were killed; two of the crew escaped; Ruiz and Montez were made prison-

John Warner Barber engraved *Death of Capt. Ferrer, the Captain of the Amistad, July, 1839* for his book *A History of the Amistad Captives*, which was published in 1840.

Many rebellions took place aboard slave ships. One of the most remarkable is the one that occurred aboard the Amistad *(Spanish for "friendship") in 1839. The slaves onboard the ship had been purchased in Havana, Cuba, and were being transported to Puerto Principe to be resold. Led by an African named Sengbe (pronounced Sin'gway), the slaves broke free of their chains and armed themselves with knives. They killed the captain and the cook and demanded to be returned to Africa. However, the Africans' captors tricked them and sailed the ship to an American port where the Africans were arrested. They were jailed, and there was a trial that lasted for many years. The Africans, including Sengbe, were finally freed and were returned to Africa.*

and girls were often singled out for special abuse. Some Africans rebelled against their captors aboard the ships and fought for their freedom. Such rebellions are commonly called insurrections. Millions of captured Africans are estimated to have died either during revolt, from illness, or from committing suicide by jumping overboard before reaching the ships' destinations.

One historian wrote that during the Middle Passage, Phillis probably "lived under the constant threat of being punished, whipped, or even killed" for disobedience. He noted that to avoid being beaten, "slaves who became spontaneously seasick—most of them had never seen the sea before in their lives—would try vainly to regulate their vomiting. Defiantly, some slaves would try to starve themselves to death." He described other horrors that were unendurable for even the strongest adults, let alone for a small child in fragile health, such as Phillis.

During the Middle Passage, ships sometimes made stops in the West Indies and in other places before traveling on to America. The voyage sometimes lasted for months. It is not known exactly how long it took Phillis to reach Boston. She was just a child when she was stolen from her family. This early separation might have been why she is reported to have had only one memory of her home. She remembered only her mother's "custom of pouring out water before the sun at his rising." Africans from some regions believed that their

TO BE SOLD on board the Ship *Bance-Island*, on tuesday the 6th of *May* next, at *Ashley-Ferry*; a choice cargo of about 250 fine healthy

NEGROES,

just arrived from the Windward & Rice Coast. —The utmost care has already been taken, and shall be continued, to keep them free from the least danger of being infected with the SMALL-POX, no boat having been on board, and all other communication with people from *Charles-Town* prevented.
Austin, Laurens, & Appleby.

N. B. Full one Half of the above Negroes have had the SMALL-POX in their own Country.

This is a newspaper advertisement from around 1780, offering slaves for sale. Its matter-of-fact tone reveals that, at the time of the advertisement's printing, slavery was an accepted part of society.

creator resided in the Sun. Therefore, this custom might have been a religious ritual that Phillis Wheatley's mother performed as an offering to honor the creator.

When slave ships reached American ports, their captives were usually sold at public auctions and at slave markets. The advertisements describing the slaves that were for sale appeared in local newspapers. Auctions and slave markets were conducted in towns in any wide open space.

Margaretta Matilda Odell, believed to be a great-grandniece of Susannah Wheatley, Phillis Wheatley's owner, published *Memoir and Poems of Phillis Wheatley, A Native African and a Slave* in 1834, and dedicated it to the "Friends of the Africans." In *Memoir*, Odell described Phillis at her arrival at the slave market as a "poor, naked child" with "no other covering than a quantity of dirty carpet about her." She said that Susannah Wheatley took pity on Phillis and chose her from among healthier, more robust-looking children.

Someone else remembered that "Aunt Wheatley was in want of a domestic. She went aboard to purchase. In looking through the ship's company of living freight, her attention was drawn to that of a slender, frail, female child, which at once enlisted her sympathies. Owing to the frailty of the child, she procured her for a trifle." In other words, Susannah Wheatley did not have to pay much money for Phillis because she was sickly, and the slave trader simply wanted to get her off his hands.

Although Phillis remembered almost nothing about her homeland, many other captured Africans remembered theirs. After they escaped or were freed by their owners, some of them wrote down their stories or told them to people who transferred them to paper. They described their lives in Africa before they were kidnapped, their hardships during the Middle Passage, and their lives as slaves. These writings and oral stories, known as slave narratives, came to be thought of as the start of an African American literary tradition. The narratives included poems by Lucy Terry, Jupiter Hammon, and Phillis Wheatley, all of whom had been slaves.

Lucy Terry's only existing poem, "Bars Fight," a ballad, tells the story of a Native American attack on white settlers in Deerfield, Massachusetts, where Terry was the property of Ebenezer Wells. She wrote the poem soon after the Deerfield Massacre occurred in 1740. It was probably recited orally many times, but it was not published for more than a century. Former slave Jupiter Hammon had published a religious poem in 1760, the year before Phillis arrived in Boston. A fourteen-page pamphlet on the slave experiences of Briton Hammon, written by himself, was published in 1760, as well. Briton Hammon was not related to Jupiter Hammon.

Individual slaves were sometimes freed by their owners during this time, and Massachusetts abolished slavery in 1783. However, the Thirteenth Amendment to the U.S. Constitution, abolishing slavery, would not come until 1865. The writings of enslaved black people were useful in the ongoing abolition movement because literacy—the ability to read and write—showed that blacks were intelligent human beings and that they deserved to be free. Of the writers' contributions mentioned earlier, Phillis Wheatley's were perhaps the most significant.

Because black people were considered to be inferior and inhuman, and without the ability to learn, Phillis was forced to undergo an oral examination by eighteen prominent white men of Boston to prove that she had indeed written the poems she claimed were hers. Her examiners included the governor and the lieutenant governor of Massachusetts, and John Hancock, Esquire, the famous first signer of the U.S. Constitution. Phillis passed the test, convincing these men that she was bright enough to be the author of her poems. They all

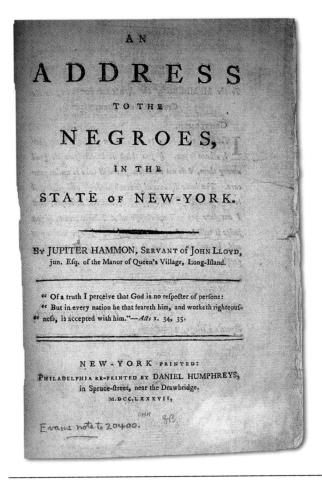

Shown here is a copy of *An Address to the Negroes in the State of New-York*, written by Jupiter Hammon, a servant of John Lloyd.

signed a letter called "To the Publick" as proof that she had been examined and was "qualified" to have written poems. This letter was included at the front of her book of poems when it was published, and thus began Phillis Wheatley's career as the Sable Muse.

2. A Long Way from Home

The Senegambia region, where it is believed Phillis was born, is a vast area in western Africa. It is watered by the Senegal and Gambia Rivers. In the eighteenth century, it was part of the area where the largest slave-trading centers were located. Historical records show that from 2,000 to 3,500 slaves were exported from this area each year. The largest number of these slave exports consisted of young African males. They were in demand to work in tobacco, sugarcane, and eventually cotton fields, as well as in other forced labors. They were also needed for the labor for which their African region was known: iron working and rice cultivation. Because these young men were taken from their homes in such large numbers, the Senegambian population suffered and so did the quality of African life.

Opposite: Ian Elwe made this 1742 map of the west coast of Africa, where Europeans built dozens of forts to serve as slave-trading posts in the eighteenth century.

Cap Bojador

Sur l'Isle

C. d'Arca

Pays de Liu daye

les Hilèles Arabes

les Beni Arabes

les Burbus Arabes

les Cere

ou des Ludayes

de 80 mille combatans

les Vled Arramena

les G

Baye des Rougets
P. de Meden

Angra dos Cavallos

les Duleim Arabes

Tesset

LE S

I. aux Herons

au nombre de mille combatans meslez avec les Zanhaga

Deserts

LES G
ou GUANA

Oulets de Line Arabes

R

s Barbes

Rade d'Angre ou l'on trafique de la poudre d'Or

Les Derveches

Pays de Tagazel

SOUDAN

Rochers blancs

Caraoli Villa de Maures

habitation des Benays

Taragarel ou Tagazel

Salines d'Ar

ROYAUME de GUALATA

Roches de Tegasa d'ou l'on ti du Sel dont se chargent les Caravanes de Maroc et de Tor

Arguin

les Lydayes

habité par les BENAYS

Guaden ou Haben

ROYAUME DE SENEGA

ou DES ZANHAGA

Desert de Tegasa

Bois ou l'on cueille la gome

Moussar Rave

Azgar Partie du Desert de Barbarie ainsi nommée par les Arabes parcequ'elle est marecageuse

ROYA

Anterote

Nayerou Quede

Grand Lac de Cavar

ou DE

Ingurbel Village de Brak

Petit Lac de Cavar

le Terrier Rouge

d'ou l'on etain

R. D'OUAILE
ou de BRAK

Lak de Panuefoule

hieurt ou Langueul boul

ROYAU. DES FOULES

Donquel le Petit Rocher

Condé

Residence de Chieratik

Tombut

Toto R.

Residence de Lamptor

Residence de Grand Jalose

Pays de Tor

CHIE RATIK

Gens de Here ou Fugitifs

Felu ou Grand rocher qui fait le Sault du Senegal

Galama

ayor

R. DES JALOFES

Dolole Bapalet

Butel

Logo

Casson

Cou
Boromay

R. des Barbecins

Combo

Dembacane

Paramanie

GALAM R.

R. Blanche

Sabaa

Na bitation de seconde

Selico

Gniamina

Bougnalem

Saraco

Congourou
Foules de C

Mandingues

Tinda

le Grand Cassan

Les

Loutou
Naquivuca

meslez a

I. des Elephans

Petit Cassan

Diacara Cunora

Contoye

Conjour

Cagnon

Malincop
Saraco

Fort de Macane

Farin troco
mines d'or

Bonda

Tanbaora

R. Noire

les Bajoque

Bagnous

Boila

R. Farin ou s Dimingue

Bamboe ou Bamboc

Congourou dougou R.
mines d'or

Fonté Guiallon ou

Cache

Gesse

mines d'or de Mandinga

Concoudougou
mines d'or

Farim

Pays naturel des Foule

Madade

Gesre Riv.

Beledougon

Grand Lac

Guinala

Courbaly Riv.

ROYAUME DE MANINGA

ou de Maninga habité par les Sousos

Guiara

Diaca

inalous
Mallous

R. DE MELLI

R. de Bitouin depend de Melli

Songo Capitale du Roy. de Mandinga

R. D'ASIA
ou d'I

les Feloupes

SERRELIONE

Conde Quojas ou Hauts Quojas

Uxco

Caceres Anguines

oles

Pays de Hondo

les Gala

HAUTE GUINÉE

Serrelione

Boulon

COTE DE MA

Dogo

R. de MANOU

Famba

COTE

This woodcut shows slaves in a cotton field, where they worked long hours, often in terrible heat. After picking the cotton, the slaves ran it through a machine called a cotton gin. The gin, invented about a decade after Phillis Wheatley's death, led to a bigger demand for slaves.

Family life was very important to Africans. Many African men had several wives at one time. This kind of marriage is called polygamy. Large extended families or clans were common. Men who fathered many children were held in high esteem by the community. Women who gave birth to many children were also valued. If Phillis had remained in Africa, she probably would have been expected to marry early, as soon as she was old enough to have children. The number of wives and children that a man had helped to build his reputation in a tribe that followed a patriarchal system, or a system in which all members of the family are descended from the same male ancestor.

Making general statements about life in as large a region of Africa as the Senegambia might lead to misconceptions, because the area is made up of many different tribes. However, polygamy existed almost everywhere, and the number of wives a man could have was partly determined by religion. In early western Africa, different tribes might have shared ideas about ancestor worship or a creator spirit, as well as about charms and rituals connected with magic. Later some tribes accepted Islam as their religion and others rejected it, preferring to continue their traditional tribal practices. Christianity was introduced by missionaries, but again many Africans were slow to accept it. The one memory Phillis retained, her mother pouring out water before the Sun came up, suggests that her family may still have been practicing their tribal religion at the time she was kidnapped.

Agriculture was considered one of the noblest kinds of work a family could do. Families' work determined their status in society, or whether they were highly regarded or not. Weaving, basket making, woodworking, toolmaking, and fishing are just a few of the other occupations that were considered highly developed skills.

More than likely, with so much time spent cultivating the land and performing other kinds of labor, there was not much time for leisure activity. However, the

This photograph of people playing a game of mankala was taken by Richard Beatty in eastern Africa, in a town called Illaut.

The board game known as mankala is perhaps one of the oldest in the world. It is believed to have originated in Egypt and then to have spread throughout the continent. Today this game is played in many different countries. Some historians believe that captured Africans brought this game with them to America. Many variations of the game exist, and there are different names for the variations. The object of the game is to capture the opponent's pieces and thereby increase the number of one's own pieces. Although some people believe that the object of capturing the opponent's pieces shows the importance to Africans of accumulating family property, many educators now believe that this game is an example of one of the ways in which Africans used mathematics.

board game known as mankala has been traced back to Africa, to a time long before Africans had any contact with Europeans. Opinions vary about who played this game, ranging from the belief that in some groups only royalty played mankala to the belief that it was played by Africans from all walks of life.

Phillis's life as a slave in Boston was no doubt very different from what it might have been in Africa. Had she remained in her homeland, she might not have written poetry in the way that she came to write it—if she wrote at all. Although African art flourished in forms such as sculpture, ornamental pottery, jewelry, tapestry, architecture, and music, African history remained primarily oral, or spoken. Phillis's life in Boston was probably also quite different from what it might have been had she been a slave in the South. In New England, slaves were owned mostly by ministers, doctors, and wealthy merchants. Although there was no shortage of menial jobs, the majority of enslaved Africans in New England probably performed

This brass head, named the *Queen Mother,* is an example of African art from the sixteenth century. It was given to the British Museum in 1897.

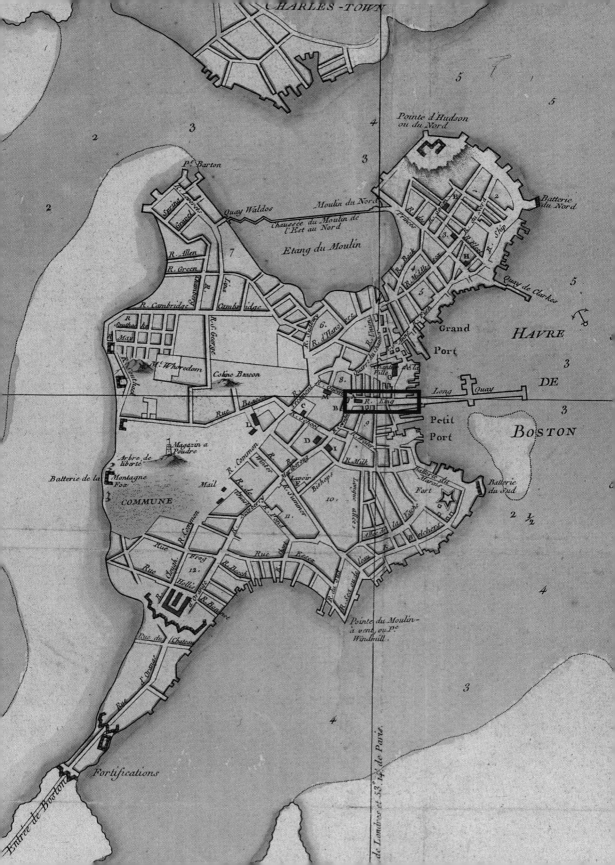

household duties and held skilled jobs in carpentry, tailoring, baking, ironworking, rope making, and the like. This does not mean that slavery was a desirable state to be in, even in the North. Life there might have been a bit easier for some, but enslaved blacks were still stripped of their African roots and their freedom. Everything they did was for the comfort of their masters' families and not for their own. Some slaves were brutally treated. Few were treated as well as Phillis Wheatley.

In a letter to a friend, Phillis herself wrote that she was treated more like Susannah Wheatley's child than like her servant. In the Wheatley household, Phillis was allowed to learn. Susannah and John Wheatley immediately noticed the girl's intelligence and allowed their eighteen-year-old daughter, Mary, to tutor her in English, in Latin, and in the Bible. She also learned "astronomy, ancient and modern geography, and ancient history." John Wheatley would write, in a letter to the publishers of Phillis's book *Poems on Various Subjects, Religious and Moral*, that she "in sixteen Months Time from her Arrival, attained the English language, to which she was an utter Stranger before," and that she could read "the most difficult Parts of the Sacred Writings, to the great Astonishment of all who heard

Opposite: Jacques Nicolas Bellin created this plan of Boston around 1764. As one of America's earliest port cities, Boston became very active in the slave trade in the 1670s. By the 1800s, however, it had become an international center for abolitionism, a movement to end slavery. King Street is outlined in blue.

The following is a Copy of a LETTER *sent by the Author's Master to the Publisher.*

PHILLIS was brought from *Africa* to *America*, in the year 1761, between seven and eight years of age. Without any assistance from school education, and by only what she was taught in the family, she, in sixteen months time from her arrival, attained the English Language, to which she was an utter stranger before, to such a degree, as to read any, the most difficult parts, of the sacred writings, to the great astonishment of all who heard her.

As to her WRITING, her own curiosity led her to it; and this she learnt in so short a time, that in the year 1765, she wrote a Letter to the Rev. Mr. OC-COM, the *Indian* minister, while in *England*.

She has a great inclination to learn the Latin tongue, and has made some progress in it. This relation is given by her Master who bought her, and with whom she now lives.

JOHN WHEATLEY,

Boston, November 14, 1772.

John Wheatley's letter to Phillis Wheatley's publisher was printed in her first book of poetry. Many people did not believe that Africans were capable of learning. He wrote the letter to provide proof that Phillis Wheatley had really written the poems in the book.

her." John Wheatley also described in this letter how quickly Phillis had learned to write, and he noted her eagerness to learn Latin.

Phillis apparently did perform some household chores. One task that is mentioned specifically in the headnote to her first published poem is "tending Table" during the visit of some guests. Margaretta Matilda Odell wrote in *Memoir* that Susannah Wheatley "would sometimes allow her [Phillis] to polish a table or dust an apartment." However, the Wheatleys must not have assigned her many domestic tasks. Instead they "supplied her with paper and pencil by her bedside to accommodate any nighttime inspiration for her verse writing."

The Old South Church was founded about 300 years ago in Boston. Originally called the Old South Meeting House, the Old South Church was born when some church members in the late 1600s broke away to start their own congregation at a new location. The Meeting House was the site of fierce political debates in the years before the American Revolution (1775-1783). It was from the Old South Meeting House that, in 1773, Samuel Adams led angry colonists to Boston Harbor to dump highly taxed tea into the water. This famous protest against the British government became known as the Boston Tea Party.

This photograph of Boston's Old South Meeting House was taken around 1900. As a meeting place and a home for free speech, the building has been in continuous use for more than 250 years.

Religion was an important part of Phillis's education from the start, because the Wheatleys were devout Christians. Mrs. Wheatley might have encouraged her slave to become literate so that Phillis could read the Bible to her, which Phillis is reported to have done quite often. Not only was she taught to read the Bible, but she was also allowed to attend church. On August 18, 1771, Phillis Wheatley was baptized and became a member of the Old South Church, formerly called the Old South Meeting House. It was not the church that the Wheatley family attended. However, it was the same church where one of America's founding fathers, Benjamin Franklin, was baptized and where the Boston Tea Party, which occurred on December 16, 1773, was organized.

Some historians have written that Phillis's membership was an exception to the rule, because slaves were not usually allowed to be baptized into the church.

However, William H. Robinson, a literary historian who has studied and written a great deal about Phillis Wheatley, believes that it was the Old South Church's practice to list black people in its catalogue of members by a single name, as "Phillis" is listed. If so, then there were several other black members who were baptized before her.

Robinson noted that Phillis and other black people could be baptized only "after the divine Service" was concluded. In other words, they were not baptized with white people. Undoubtedly, Phillis also had to sit in the section of the church intended for black people, whether that was in the rear of the first floor or in the gallery of the second floor. However kindly the Wheatleys and their friends treated Phillis Wheatley, in society's eyes she was still a slave, so she did not have the same privileges as whites.

3. A Colonial Education

During the seventeenth and eighteenth centuries, the most widely used schoolbook in America was *The New England Primer*, also called the Little Bible. It combined Bible teachings with the study of the alphabet by introducing each letter, *A* through *Z*, at the beginning of a religious phrase.

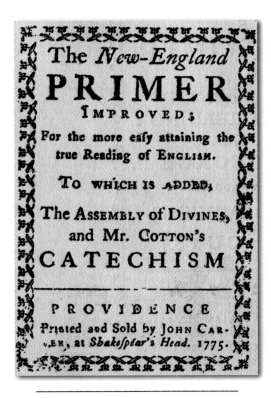

The New England Primer, a very popular elementary textbook in colonial America, was used in both public and private schools.

This schoolbook also contained questions and answers about God and Christianity. The familiar children's prayer beginning "Now I lay me down to sleep" was first printed in this book. Very likely this is the schoolbook that the Wheatley twins, Mary and Nathaniel, used to learn to

The New England Primer
was first printed in Boston in
1690 by Benjamin Harris. This was
the book from which most children of
colonial America learned to read.
It was used into the nineteenth
century and is said to have sold
millions of copies.

read, and, at the same time, to learn about religion. In the 1700s, schools were strongly influenced by religion. In fact, the first educational institutions were established primarily for the purpose of teaching the "principles of religion."

Through books such as *The New England Primer*, children were taught prayers and moral lessons. The moral lessons provided examples of good Christian behavior and bad behavior, along with examples of the rewards and punishments that might be the consequences of a person's actions. Children were taught specifically that a person's main purpose in life is to glorify God, that there is only one God, and that any kind of wrongdoing is a sin against God. The effect of such religious lessons on Phillis Wheatley was demonstrated not only in the poetry she wrote but also in her habit of exhibiting very proper behavior. Odell stressed in *Memoir* that Phillis possessed a "meekness of spirit," and that "she was very gentle-tempered" and "extremely affectionate."

Phillis Wheatley did not attend a formal school. She learned from the examples set in the Wheatley home. Susannah Wheatley is said to have had "a passion for the spellbinding sermon," and the Wheatleys' friends and acquaintances included a number of ministers. It is not surprising that, in tutoring Phillis, Mary Wheatley made Bible study a big part of Phillis's experience of learning to read and write. This alone was enough to make Phillis stand out from other blacks. Learning Latin language and Latin literature placed her far ahead of most people, black or white. Whether or not white children received a formal education—that is, whether or not they attended school—depended on their parents' social and financial status. If children were needed to work at home, they could not attend school regularly. Children from very poor families were rarely able to attend school at all. It was fortunate for Phillis not only that both Mary and Nathaniel had been so well educated, but also that they were willing to tutor her. Education was not an opportunity often granted to slaves. As time went on and the institution of slavery became more firmly established, it even became illegal in some states to teach slaves to read and to write. Luckily for Phillis, this was not the case when she was being tutored in Massachusetts.

The small, frail girl from Africa was a willing and an able pupil. In less than two years of her arrival into the Wheatley household, she became fluent in a language that was very different from her own. She also soon learned geography, history, and astronomy, in addition to learning about English and Latin literature and about the Bible. When she began to write poetry, her mistress, Mrs. Susannah Wheatley, encouraged and promoted her work. She made sure Phillis was comfortable at home by allowing her to have a fire on cold nights and to burn a candle in her room all night. She also arranged for Phillis's visits to the homes of prominent Bostonians, who visited her in return. One time a representative of the earl of Dartmouth visited Phillis to see firsthand the "very extraordinary female Slave." He said, "I was astonish'd, and could hardly believe my own Eyes. I was present while she wrote."

Phillis's accomplishments might have been astonishing to people like the earl's representative not only because she was an African who could learn so quickly, but also because the quality of her education was extraordinary. As history books describe it, she was better educated than were most white women of her time, even those from elite families. Phillis Wheatley had learned Latin language and Latin literature so

Sir Joshua Reynolds painted this portrait of William Legge (1731–1801), the second earl of Dartmouth, around 1757. Legge was a British statesman who opposed the Stamp Act, a tax imposed on the colonists by the British.

well that she was able to translate the well-known Roman poet Ovid's story of Niobe, from *Metamorphoses VI*. Prominent townspeople were so impressed by her achievements that they visited and encouraged her. They would lend Phillis Wheatley books and would give her some as presents.

The Wheatleys treated Phillis very kindly and gave her opportunities that were unusual for a slave. However, Mrs. Wheatley occasionally put her slave on display as a curiosity, asking Phillis to recite her poetry for visitors. It can be argued that Susannah Wheatley was simply showing her off as a proud parent shows off a talented child. However, Susannah treated Phillis as a curiosity in other ways. For example, Susannah

Wheatley tried to keep Phillis from having close contact with other slaves owned by the family. Mrs. Wheatley is said to have scolded her slave Prince once for daring to sit beside Phillis while bringing her home in the family chaise, or carriage, from a visit in town. Although this story has been handed down as a humorous one, it demonstrates the peculiar, indeed, the contradictory behavior of

This restored fresco of Ovid was originally created in Italy between 1500 and 1503. Ovid was a Roman poet who enjoyed widespread fame for his work and who knew the emperor Augustus.

some slave owners. The Wheatleys treated Phillis like one of the family, so it seems strange that they waited many years before granting her freedom.

Throughout Phillis's life, it was often that she was a slave who was able to write poetry, rather than the poetry itself, that was the subject of discussion. Many viewed Phillis Wheatley as a curiosity, rather than as a gifted poet. As with the eighteen Bostonian men who examined Phillis to ascertain whether or not she was capable of writing poetry, many prominent white people wrote with admiration and astonishment that an African, a slave, could perform such a feat. A review in a London periodical stated that her poems were not particularly powerful, but that they caused surprise and admiration because they were written by a "young untutored African."

Some people criticized Phillis simply because of her color. The most famous of these critics was stateman and patriot Thomas Jefferson, who made uncomplimentary statements about her "silly poems" and her "sable generation," as well as her African background. The truth is that Thomas Jefferson, unfortunately, believed in the superiority of white people over blacks in both

Thomas Jefferson, as shown in this 1805 portrait by Rembrandt Peale, was the third president of the United States and the main author of the Declaration of Independence.

physical appearance and in intelligence. In his *Notes on the State of Virginia*, Jefferson wrote that the "fine mixture of red and white" skin, the "flowing hair," and "a more elegant symmetry of form" were characteristics that made white people more beautiful than blacks. He believed black people to be "dull," with no imagination or capacity for real love. He thought that blacks' inferiority was a natural condition and not a result of their "condition of life." With regard to the creative abilities of Phillis Wheatley or any other black person, he wrote, "Among the blacks is misery enough, God knows, but no poetry."

In the years to come, Phillis Wheatley's remarkable education and aptitude for learning would be what people discussed most about her. Both blacks and whites would hold her up as an example in the argument for blacks' humanity and the abolition of slavery.

In *Notes on the State of Virginia*, Thomas Jefferson discusses the land and the people of Virginia and his views on America's future. His book reveals his prejudice against blacks.

4. Journey to Freedom

Despite people's disagreements about whether an African female slave could or should write poetry, Susannah Wheatley continued to encourage and to promote Phillis, and Phillis kept writing. Whatever other motivations Susannah Wheatley might have had for assisting Phillis, it is clear that she had come to look upon Phillis Wheatley as a "beloved protégé." Susannah Wheatley was largely responsible for the publicity and the financial help necessary to promote Phillis's poetry. Because of her mistress's efforts, Phillis's poems began to appear in a wide variety of newspapers, magazines, pamphlets, and broadsides.

Phillis's poem "On the Death of the Rev. Mr. George Whitefield. 1770" was widely and repeatedly published in America. In the following year, it was also published in London. Phillis might have been aware that Reverend Whitefield, for whom she wrote this elegy of praise, owned slaves. Almost every white person who could afford to do so owned them. However, Reverend Whitefield publicly spoke out against the ill treatment of slaves, and he also spoke of establishing a school for free blacks. He was part of the missionary movement whose members believed in blacks being educated. For one thing, it meant they would be able to read the Bible. In the poem that Phillis wrote about him, she praised him for his fiery preaching and his ability to "inflame" people's hearts and minds. Perhaps Phillis thought he had been able to inflame the hearts and minds of other slaveholders, thereby encouraging them to stop the brutal treatment of enslaved Africans.

George Whitefield helped to stimulate a Protestant revival in Britain and in the American colonies through his religious speeches.

Susannah Wheatley's high regard for Reverend Whitefield and others like him in the missionary movement might have been yet another factor in her decision to educate Phillis. The Wheatleys would have known of Reverend Whitefield's reputation as a radical evangelist and a leading figure in the Great Awakening, which was a religious revival that took place during the eighteenth

This illustration, published in an 1865 book titled *The History of New England*, shows a singing procession in 1740 in New England.Group song and prayer in public were common during the Great Awakening, a period of religious revival.

century. An interesting story has been handed down over the years about Reverend Whitefield's fiery sermons and his ability to stir up an audience of believers. As the story goes, the reverend was a guest speaker at the New South Church in Boston, where the Wheatleys were members. While preaching one of his sermons, he caused so much excitement among the congregation that five people were trampled to death. Perhaps Susannah and John Wheatley were there on that Sunday morning in September 1740, and perhaps the

Reverend Whitefield story was one that got repeated so often that eventually Phillis and the Wheatley children heard it. So accustomed was Phillis to being included in the family circle that she probably heard many such stories, which might have provided material for her poems.

Phillis might have written about Whitefield at the urging of Susannah Wheatley. Undoubtedly, it was at Mrs. Wheatley's suggestion that Phillis sent the poem about Whitefield to Selina Hastings, the countess of Huntingdon. The poem, along with a letter written by Phillis, sparked the countess' interest, because Reverend Whitefield had been her chaplain, and also because both Whitefield and the countess were known for befriending and supporting Africans.

In 1772, when Phillis's attempt to have a book of her poems published in Boston was unsuccessful, Susannah Wheatley enlisted the aid of Captain Robert Calef to help get the book published in London. Calef was a Wheatley family friend and the commander of the Wheatleys' ship, the *London Packet*, which sailed regularly between Boston and London. His own home and family ties were in Homerton, which is near London. On behalf of Susannah Wheatley, Calef contacted Archibald Bell, a London bookseller, who accepted the book for publication. Calef and Bell then sought permission to dedicate the book to the countess of Huntingdon. The appearance of her name in the book would help to increase its recognition and its sales. The

This portrait of Selina Hastings, the countess of Huntingdon,
was painted around 1770. Hastings was a central figure in the revival
of Methodism, a kind of Christianity, in eighteenth-century Britain.
She built chapels and helped to pay for the training of clergymen.

The portrait of Phillis Wheatley that was included in her 1773 collection of poems is believed to have been painted by Scipio Moorhead, an African slave in America. Scipio worked for the Boston minister John Moorhead, a neighbor and a friend of the Wheatley family.

countess agreed to the dedication and insisted that the poet's picture be included as the frontispiece. Not only was Phillis's picture provided for the book, but it was also made available for sale separately.

It is believed that Mrs. Wheatley hired the slave Scipio Moorhead to paint what would become the most widely known picture of Phillis. Phillis wrote a poem as a tribute to him entitled "To S. M. A Young African Painter, On Seeing His Works." She took every opportunity to praise the work of other blacks.

Next Spread: Poems on Various Subjects, Religious and Moral is Phillis Wheatley's only published book and the first volume of poetry to be published by an African American. After her book was printed in 1773, Wheatley's reputation spread in Europe and in America.

PHILLIS WHEATLEY, NEGRO SERVANT to Mr JOHN WHEATLEY, of BOSTON.

POEMS

ON

VARIOUS SUBJECTS,

RELIGIOUS AND MORAL.

BY

PHILLIS WHEATLEY,

NEGRO SERVANT to Mr. JOHN WHEATLEY,
of BOSTON, in NEW ENGLAND.

LONDON:

Printed for A. BELL, Bookseller, Aldgate; and sold by
Messrs. COX and BERRY, King-Street, BOSTON.

MDCCLXXIII.

This portrait showing Wheatley dressed in a gown and jewels appeared in *Revue des Colonies* in Paris between 1834 and 1842. Believed to be based on a W. E. Braxton print, it is a rare depiction of Phillis, whose mistress insisted that she dress plainly.

At about this same time, the asthmatic condition from which Phillis had always suffered caused the Wheatleys' doctors so much alarm that they prescribed a sea trip for her recuperation. They believed that the fresh sea air would be good for her. Through the eighteenth and nineteenth centuries, people assumed that disease was caused in part by bad air. In May 1773, Phillis Wheatley sailed for London, England, on the *London Packet* in the company of Nathaniel Wheatley, who was going there on business. Although Phillis was traveling to London for her health, Susannah Wheatley saw it as an excellent opportunity for her to gain publicity. The news of Phillis's departure was printed in many newspapers throughout New England, New York, and Pennsylvania along with a poem she wrote, titled "A Farewel to America." The poem tells of Phillis sailing from America to England and of her sadness in leaving her beloved mistress.

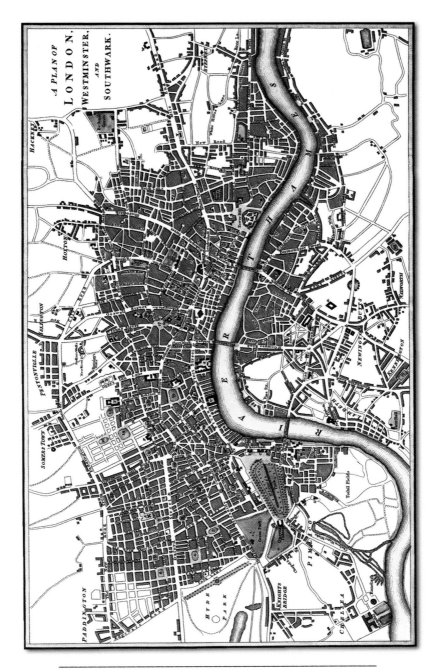

B. Baker created this map of London. Phillis Wheatley's
trip to London in 1773 served to improve her health
and to stir up publicity for her soon-to-be-published book.

Newspaper accounts appeared before and after her departure through the efforts of Susannah Wheatley. They usually referred to Phillis as the "extraordinary" or the "ingeneous negro poet." The attention must have been exciting for Phillis, but it raises the question of how she felt about the constant references to her race. It is safe to guess that she made no outward show of annoyance, even if she felt it. She was known to behave in a manner appropriate to her station in life and in accordance with her Christian beliefs. In fact, in her own poems and letters, Phillis often referred to her race. Today it is believed that this was one way she sought to bring attention to and to further the cause of abolition.

The trip to London occurred at the same time that preparations were being made for the publication of Phillis's book. On the ship, a great fuss was made over Phillis. After arriving in London, she was very well received by many important people. Brook Watson, who became lord mayor of London, gave her a copy of John Milton's long epic poem, *Paradise Lost*. Phillis wrote to a friend, with much excitement, that she had spent almost half an hour in conversation with William, earl of Dartmouth. He gave her five guineas with which to buy a collection of poetry by Alexander Pope, the eighteenth-century British poet whom she admired and whose poetry many felt she imitated in her own work. The American statesman Benjamin Franklin, who was in London at the same time, later wrote that he had visited

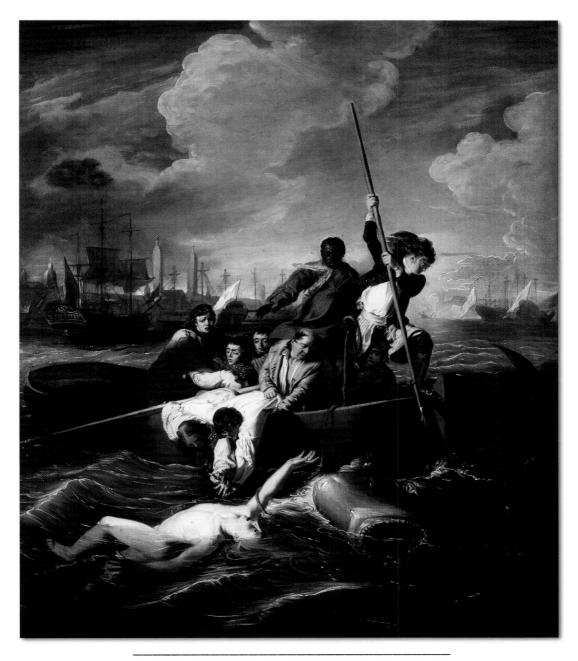

Brook Watson was the subject of John Singleton Copley's 1782 painting
Watson and the Shark. In 1749, fourteen-year-old Watson, serving as a
crew member on a ship, was attacked by a shark while swimming.
Fortunately, his shipmates were able to rescue him.

This portrait of Benjamin Franklin (1706–1790) was created by Joseph-Siffred Duplessis. Franklin was an American patriot, a scientist, a writer, and an inventor.

her there and had offered his services to her. Sometime after the trip, Franklin wrote to his nephew-in-law that he, Franklin, must have offended Nathaniel Wheatley by calling to see Phillis and not first asking to see Nathaniel. The countess of Huntingdon was in poor health and could not see Phillis in London, but she invited Phillis to her estate in southern Wales. It is believed that some other influential people Phillis met in London tried to arrange for her to be presented to King George III.

The poems to be included in Phillis Wheatley's book were mostly about people and events important to Boston, but she also made sure that some of them were of interest to her English audience. She changed some titles and content to make them more appropriate and deleted poems if they were too critical of British people and their country. She also added the newly written "Farewel to America." Because of the times in which she lived and her position as a woman and a slave, it is not realistic to think

This is an undated portrait, by Sir Joshua Reynolds, of George III, king of Britain. The king opposed the American colonists' bid for independence.

that Phillis's poetry went uncensored. Censoring means that someone in a position of authority made changes to Phillis Wheatley's poems without asking her permission and sometimes without her knowledge before they were printed. This was not the same as Phillis changing and correcting her own work, which she often did. Nor was it the same as someone simply correcting misspellings or mistakes. Controversial or offensive poems would not have gotten published. This may be why her feelings about slavery are so carefully worded or are expressed indirectly in her poems.

Whether she wrote for her American audience or for her English one, the religious themes in her poetry did not change. Her poems were usually concerned with God, heaven, and the human soul. She wrote about freedom and equality in heaven. Many of her poems have a moral, which means they aim to make a statement about right and wrong.

In one of her most well known poems, "On Being Brought From Africa to America," she writes of how fortunate she was to have been brought out of pagan Africa. Many people have criticized her for saying this, because she was kidnapped and was brought into slavery. Through her poem "On Being Brought From Africa to America," Phillis Wheatley wanted to make a moral point about Christianity. By stressing that skin color does not matter in heaven because all are equal in the eyes of God, she meant to give black people hope and to suggest to whites that they had done something wrong.

Some have called Phillis Wheatley an "occasional" poet. This means that she wrote poetry for specific occasions, usually fitting the topics of her poetry into existing or what can be called traditional patterns. For example, she wrote many elegies, which are poems that reflect either on the death of friends and celebrated people or on death itself. Religious principles were important in the elegies she wrote, because she would usually praise the departed person's virtues and describe his or her definite reception into heaven. She has been criticized for writing about the deaths of people who did not mean anything to her. However, these critics did not understand the personal importance to Phillis of some people whose deaths she wrote about, or therefore the significance of these poems to her. "An Elegy to Dr. Samuel Cooper," for example, was written in memory of the man who baptized her.

This is Phillis Wheatley's most well known poem. It is the poem that is usually included in most American poetry books. It is controversial because, if read too literally, Africa seems to be depicted negatively:

'Twas mercy brought me from my *Pagan* land,
Taught my benighted soul to understand
That there's a God, that there's a *Saviour* too:
Once I redemption neither sought nor knew.
Some view our sable race with scornful eye,
"Their colour is a diabolic die."
Remember, *Christians*, *Negros*, black as *Cain*,
May be refin'd, and join th' angelic train.

—*Phillis Wheatley*
"On Being Brought From Africa to America"

Just as Phillis was not free of censorship, she also was not completely free to choose what or even how she would write. Sometimes she was asked to write particular poems in praise of well-known people by the people themselves, and other poems were written at the urging of her mistress. In addition, her poetry had to conform to the required decorum of the day. The world of literature called for a certain amount of formality and dignity. It was also a world dominated by white men. Phillis was required to be extremely humble because she was a Christian, a black person, and a woman. When the physician Benjamin Rush praised her in his antislavery writings, one of the things he pointed out was that her accomplishments "do honor to her sex." She always had to be mindful of the fact that many people's eyes were upon her, and she could not risk writing anything that would shame or bring scorn to the Wheatleys, herself, or African people.

It was Phillis Wheatley's observance of the decorum of the day and the religious focus of her poetry that most caught the attention and the praise of the countess of Huntingdon. This led the countess to agree to support the publication of Phillis's book. Unfortunately, Phillis never got the chance to meet the countess or King George III and Queen Charlotte. She was called back to Boston, because Susannah Wheatley was very ill. Phillis left London on July 26, 1773, before the publication of her book.

In September 1773, *Poems on Various Subjects, Religious and Moral* was published in London. Phillis's book was widely publicized in London area newspapers, such as *Lloyd's Evening Post and British Chronicle*, the *Public Advertiser*, the *London Chronicle*, the *London Morning Post*, and the *Daily Advertiser*. The notices included excerpts of her poems. The book was reprinted in London at least three more times and sold approximately 1,200 copies. In sever-

Thomas Lawrence painted this portrait of Queen Charlotte in 1789. The queen gave birth to fifteen children in the first twenty-one years of her marriage to King George III.

al of the notices, British reviewers openly reproached the Wheatley family and Bostonians in general for boasting about the "talented slave poet" but not giving her freedom.

Perhaps Phillis was fortunate that Boston publishers would not publish her book, because it had made the trip to London necessary. The journey across the Atlantic for the second time in her young life came to be important for a reason apart from just getting a book published. Phillis wrote to a friend that it was the desire of her friends in England that she be given her freedom. She believed that their pressing for her freedom and the comments published in the papers persuaded her mistress to grant her freedom. Shortly after Phillis's return to Boston from London, the Wheatleys freed the young woman who had lived as a slave for twelve years.

5. Blacks and the American Revolution

On March 3, 1774, approximately six months after Phillis Wheatley was freed, Susannah Wheatley died. Although Phillis was allowed to remain in the Wheatley home, her mistress' death marked the end of the life Phillis had come to know, and, in many ways, to enjoy. At that time, Mary Wheatley had been married to the Reverend John Lathrop for three years, and the couple lived in their own Boston home. Nathaniel had remained in London as a permanent resident, marrying a well-to-do woman named Mary Enderby. The household had already undergone a number of major changes, but Susannah Wheatley's death was the one that would have the most impact on Phillis.

The increasing presence of British troops also disrupted Phillis's life and the lives of most Bostonians. Outbreaks of violence, because of unfair taxation and other acts of British power over the colonies, had been occurring for a number of years. Colonists were not represented in Parliament, which meant they had neither voice nor vote when it came to making laws about taxes

During the event referred to as the Boston Massacre, British soldiers fired at a group of Boston colonists who were waving clubs and shouting at them. Five colonists were killed. This provoked outrage against the British army in the colonies. The presence of British troops in Boston had long been a sore point among the colonists.

or other matters. They therefore believed that Parliament's forcing them to pay taxes was a violation of their liberties. Two of the most well known of these violent outbreaks in Boston were the Boston Massacre on March 5, 1770, and the Boston Tea Party on December 16, 1773. During the Boston Massacre, a brave runaway slave named Crispus Attucks was the first of five people shot and killed as he led a small group of men in an attack against some British soldiers occupying the city.

History books have recorded Crispus Attucks as the first martyr to fall in the colonists' struggle for independence from British rule. Phillis Wheatley's poem "On the

Death of Mr. Snider Murder'd by Richardson" records another person as "the first martyr for the cause." Christopher Snyder, the subject of her poem, was an eleven-year-old boy who was killed in an incident that took place before the Boston Massacre. On February 23, 1770, Snyder and a group of other young boys staged a boycott against a Boston merchant who continued to import and sell tea despite the objections of most of Boston's citizens. Ebenezer Richardson, also a merchant, tried to break up the boycott, but the boys threw stones

This undated painting by John Pufford depicts the killing of Crispus Attucks by a British soldier during the Boston Massacre on March 5, 1770. *Inset:* A newspaper article on the Boston Massacre described the funerals to be held for its victims and represented each victim with a drawing of a coffin.

at him, driving him away. He returned with a shotgun and fired into the crowd of boys, wounding one and killing young Snyder. Wheatley's poem describing the incident reflects the citizens' bitterness over the loss of this brave boy, as well as their condemnation of his murderer.

The Boston Massacre and the death of Crispus Attucks were major factors in making some of the colonists think about how wrong it was to fight for their own freedom but to deny black people theirs. Important men who had never done so before began to speak out openly against slavery. Women also made their thoughts known, although perhaps less publicly. One of these women was Abigail Adams, the wife of John Adams, the second president of the United States. Abigail Adams wrote in a letter to her husband about the injustice of fighting "ourselves for what we are daily robbing and plundering from those who have as good a right to freedom as we have." It would be a long while, however, before anything occurred to correct the injustice Abigail described in her letter.

Phillis continued to write poetry during the trying times leading to the American Revolution. Her writings continued to focus on the events and the people around her. Listed in one of her book proposals is a poem titled "On the Affray in King-Street, on the Evening of the 5th of March." It must have been written about the Boston Massacre, which happened on this date in front of the Old State House, which was on King Street not far from principle of liberty and equality is, master Heath has opend an evening school to instruct a number of Apprentices Lads cyphering at a shilling a week finding their own wood and candles.

James desired that he might go & told him to go with my compliments to master Heath and ask him if he would take him, he did & master Heath returnd for answer that he would. accordingly James went after about a week. neighbour Faxon came in one evening and requested to speak to me. his errant was to inform me that if James went to School, it would break up the school for the other Lads refused to go. pray mr Faxon has the Boy misbehaved? if he has let the master turn him out of school o no, there was no complaint of that kind, but they did not chuse to go to school with a black Boy. and why not object to going to meeting because he does mr Faxon? is there not room enough in the school for him to take his separate forme. yes. did these Lads ever object to James playing for them when at a dance, how can they bear to have a Black in the room with them there? o it is not I that object, or my Boys. it is some others, pray who are they? why did not they come themselves! this mr Faxon is attacking the principle of Liberty and equality upon the only ground upon which it ought to be supported, an equality of rights the Boy is a Freeman as much as any of the young men

---

Abigail Adams wrote at least two letters in which she discussed the rights of African Americans. In this February 13, 1797, letter, Abigail discussed the education of a freed black named James. She had sent him to attend night school but was informed that the other students did not wish to go to school with a black boy. Abigail Adams wrote, "The Boy is a Freeman as much as any of the young men."

John Trumbull painted this portrait of George Washington in military uniform in 1790. Washington is known as the father of his country.

where Phillis lived. Unfortunately there is no surviving copy of this poem. She also wrote the poem "To a Gentleman of the Navy," which was published in the *Royal American Magazine* in December 1774. This poem was probably inspired by the presence of royal officers in the Wheatley home by order of the British parliament. The poem's publication apparently inspired an anonymous poet to write the poem "The Answer," and Phillis wrote yet another poem in response to that. She also wrote her famous poem about George Washington during this time. She had been living with Mary Wheatley Lathrop and her family, who had fled Boston and had gone to Providence, Rhode Island.

As was Phillis's custom, she sent the poem she had written about George Washington to him, accompanied by a letter. In the letter, she apologized for taking the liberty of writing to such an important person, apologized for any inaccuracies in the poem, and wished him success. It was addressed to "His Excellency General Washington" and signed "Your Excellency's most obedient humble servant, Phillis Wheatley." Washington would soon become commander in chief of the Continental army, and Wheatley's poem has been called a "plea and challenge" for him to restore the country to a place of peace and freedom.

Several months later, General Washington sent a letter to Phillis apologizing for the delay in answering her, thanking her for her poem, and praising her "great poetical Talents." He wrote that he would have had her poem about him published but was afraid people would think he was just doing it to flatter himself. He addressed the letter to "Mrs. Phillis," ended it by inviting her to visit him at his headquarters in Cambridge, and signed it, "I am, with great Respect your obedient humble Servant." Although Phillis would die before George Washington became the first president of the United States, receiving such a courtesy even from an important general and statesman must have pleased her very much.

Phillis is reported to have visited George Washington in March 1776, and to have been treated courteously by the general and his staff. Although this story has been repeated over the years, there is no evidence to prove that it happened. It would not be a surprise to learn that it

13

the delay, and plead my excuse for the seeming, but not real neglect.

I thank you most sincerely for your polite notice of me, in the elegant Lines you enclosed; and however undeserving I may be of such encomium and panegyrick, the style and manner exhibit a striking proof of your great poetical Talents. In honour of which, and as a tribute justly due to you, I would have published the Poem, had I not been apprehensive, that, while I only meant to give the World this new instance of your genius, I might have incurred the imputation of Vanity. This and nothing else, determined me not to give it place in the public Prints.

If you should ever come to Cambridge, or near Head Quarters, I shall be happy to see a person so favoured by the Muses, and to whom nature has been so liberal and beneficent in her dispensations.

I am, with great Respect,
Your obedt humble servant,
G. Washington.

George Washington wrote to Phillis Wheatley on February 28, 1776, to thank her for her poem and to praise her talent. At the end of his letter, Washington wrote: "If you should ever come to Cambridge, or near Head Quarters, I shall be happy to see a person so favoured by the Muses."

did, however. Phillis was accustomed to meeting extremely important people and surely would not have hesitated to visit a general if given the opportunity. Phillis also might have visited George Washington to show her support of the patriots. The Wheatleys had counted a number of British people among their friends, but by now Phillis considered herself an American and there her loyalties

This painting, based on an illustration by George Henry Millar that was engraved by John Lodge between 1781 and 1783 for Barnard's *New Complete and Authentic History of England*, depicts the Battle of Bunker Hill, the first large-scale engagement of the Revolution. It took place on June 17, 1775, in Charlestown, Massachusetts. The losses inflicted on the British in this battle strengthened the Americans' confidence.

would lie until her death. In fact, she refused the advice of people such as Susannah Wheatley and Reverend Samson Occum, who, on occasion, suggested that Phillis return to Africa as a Christian missionary to the natives.

During the time in which Phillis Wheatley was reported to have visited George Washington, he must have been already preparing to take charge of the Continental forces. Under his command, it was decided that black men, enslaved or free, would be excluded from military service. Despite the proven bravery and loyalty of black men such as Crispus Attucks and those who had fought in the battles of Lexington, Concord, and Bunker Hill, the colonists were afraid that blacks would rebel or would simply run away if allowed into the military. Many of the colonists refused to give up their way of life, which depended greatly on slavery. In a draft of the Declaration of Independence, Thomas Jefferson listed slavery as one of the offenses of King George III. He later deleted it, because he did not want to risk the anger of those he counted on to support the larger cause. He also must have realized that he could not accuse the British of an offense of which the American colonists were also guilty.

It turned out that blacks were called to join the British army, because the British were outnumbered and desperate. In November 1775, Lord John Murray Dunmore, the royal governor of Virginia, issued a proclamation that promised blacks their freedom if they fought on the side of the British. Seeing the danger of blacks going over to the other side, George Washington then changed his order to allow black men to enlist, but only if they were already free. The

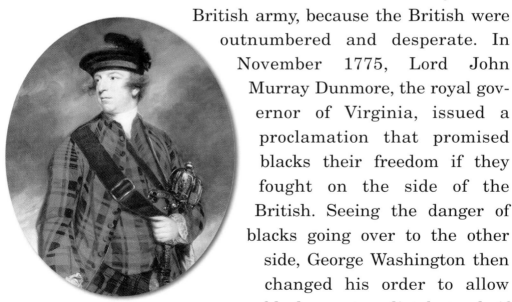

Sir Joshua Reynolds painted this portrait of John Murray, fourth earl of Dunmore.

colonists, or patriots, promised blacks "good treatment" if they joined with them. Still, many thousands of blacks who wanted their freedom ran away to British lines. Even with the help of these black men, however, the British troops eventually would be defeated, and the runaway slaves would be sent to Nova Scotia with other loyalists.

Thousands of blacks did run away simply to escape slavery, not to join the British. Other blacks, however, fought on the side of the colonists, because Washington eventually allowed slaves to fight as well. Many of these men became war heroes. Tens of thousands of them were given their freedom. Yet, when the Second Continental Congress adopted the Declaration of Independence on July 4, 1776, separating the thirteen colonies from Great Britain, slavery still existed. In January 1777, under the title of "A Great Number of Blackes," a petition was made to the "Honorable Counsel & House of Representatives for the State of Massachusetts Bay" asking for an end to slavery.

In the same year, when Major General David Wooster was killed in the American Revolution, Phillis wrote a poem not only lamenting his death and praising his brave leadership, but also openly condemning slavery. It is probably one of the only poems in which she directly speaks of the hypocrisy of one race fighting for its own freedom while holding another race in bondage. She had written similar opinions a few years earlier in

David Wooster, here in a 1776 portrait published by Thomas Hart, fought against Britain during the American Revolution. In 1775, he served as supreme commander of all U.S. troops in Canada.

a letter to the reverend Samson Occum. Like the petition to the courts by "A Great Number of Blackes," Phillis's poem stated clearly that slaves wanted to be free.

It is not clear where Phillis was living when she wrote this poem, or where she was living when John Wheatley died on March 12, 1778. All his possessions were left to his children. Phillis was not named in his will, which meant that she would have to find a way to fend for herself, if she were not already doing so. Mary Wheatley Lathrop died in September of the same year in which her father died. Nathaniel Wheatley was still living in London, too far away to be of help to Phillis, who suffered from the loss of her close friends. Her life was about to change drastically from the one she had known since being brought from Africa to America.

6. Marriage and Motherhood

Phillis had not been encouraged, at least not while Susannah Wheatley was alive, to make any friends among blacks. Even though there was a community of free blacks in Boston, in an area called New Guinea, there is no evidence that Phillis was connected to them. Her one known black friend seemed to be more like what today is called a pen pal, except perhaps their relationship was a bit closer. Phillis and Obour Tanner, an enslaved woman in Newport, Rhode Island, carried on a seven-year correspondence. In her letters to Tanner are indications that Phillis kept up with the activities of other blacks, even if she did not have much contact with them. These letters are very important today, because they provide information directly from Phillis Wheatley. According to Phillis's letters, some of the white acquaintances she had made through Susannah Wheatley were not as interested in befriending her after her mistress' death. Others had left the city with the British or had passed away. Thus early in 1778, after John Wheatley's death, Phillis found herself alone.

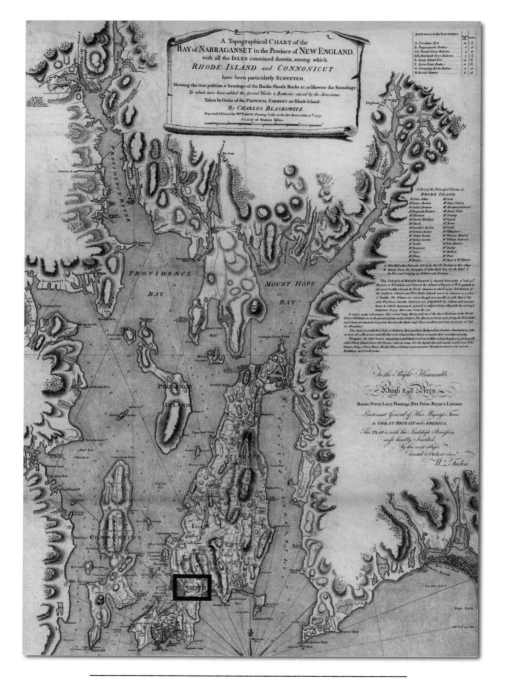

Phillis Wheatley first met her friend Obour Tanner while accompanying the Wheatley family to Newport, Rhode Island, which is outlined in blue in this 1777 map by William Faden.

It remains a mystery how and when she met John Peters, whom she married on April 1, 1778. She mentioned him in a letter to her friend Obour Tanner, dated October 30, 1773, providing evidence that she knew him for at least five years before the marriage. Under what circumstances she knew him, the letter does not say. All the accounts of John Peters agree on several points: that he was free, that he was handsome, and that he thought well of himself. Some accounts say that he tried his hand at many different occupations and had money problems. Others say he had a grocery store business in Boston and that he was very respectable, but that his business failed soon after he married Phillis. All the accounts say that Phillis's life went downhill once she married John Peters.

Phillis herself might have thought of John Peters as clever and agreeable. Others described him as intelligent and said he was a good speaker and writer. By some, he has been called "shiftless and improvident," meaning lazy and wasteful. Yet some of the more reliable sources say that he performed a variety of jobs, including legal work, such as reading about the law and appearing in Boston's courts. The reports are all so different, however, that to this day no one knows the truth.

A record of Phillis's marriage to John Peters is included in the book *Early History of Boston*. It simply gives the date of their marriage and describes them as "free Negroes," but the record proves that they were indeed married. Different stories about the couple's marriage are almost as plentiful as are those solely about John Peters. They differ not only on how the couple lived but also about where. The stories also differ about when and where their children were born and where they died. Over the years, attempts have been made to correct the misconceptions about John Peters, the Peters' marriage, and the latter portion of Phillis's life.

It seems clear that the marriage began well, with regard to the Peters' living conditions. Two pieces of evidence show that the Peters lived on a fashionable street called Queen Street for at least the first two years. First, there is Phillis's letter of May 1778, to her friend Obour Tanner, which informed her to direct future letters to Mr. John Peters on Queen Street. Also, there is a 1780 record of a considerable sum of money paid for taxes on the Queen Street house. Unfortunately, Boston was still suffering from the ravages of war. During this period, it must have been hard for anyone to make a good living. After Phillis gave birth to her first child, there was yet another person to care for. Perhaps because of the addition to their family and the various misfortunes of war, their prosperity could not last. Yet, although they might not have been thriving, there is no evidence that they suffered extreme poverty.

Meanwhile, Phillis continued to write, hoping to make some money from her poetry. In 1779, under her married name, Phillis Peters, she advertised in local papers her proposal for a second book of poems. This

Dear Obour.

I rec'd your obliging Letter, enclos'd in your rev'd Pastor's & handed me by his Son. I have lately met with a great trial in the death of my mistress. Let us imagine the loss of a Parent, Sister or Brother the tenderness of all these were united in her. — I was a poor little outcast & a stranger when she took me in, not only into her house but I presently became a sharer in her most tender affections, I was treated by her more like her child than her servant, no opportunity was left unimprov'd, of giving me the best of advice, but in terms how tender? how engaging! this I hope ever to keep in remembrance. Her example by life was a greater monitor than all her precepts and Instruction; thus we may observe of how much greater force example is than Instruction. To alleviate our sorrows we had the satisfaction to see her depart in inexpressible raptures, earnest longings & impatient thirstings for the upper Courts of the Lord. Do, my dear friend, remember me & this family in your Closet, that this afflicting dispensation may be sanctifyd to us. I am very sorry to hear that you are indisposed but hope this will find you in better health. I have been unwell the greater Part of the winter, but am much better as the Spring approaches. Pray excuse my not writing to you so long before, for I have been so busy lately. that I could not find leizure. I shall send the 5 Books you wrote for, the first convenient opportunity. if you want more, they shall be ready for you I am very affectionately your Friend

Phillis Wheatley

Boston March 21. 1774.

This letter from Phillis Wheatley to her friend Obour Tanner is dated March 21, 1774. The two corresponded for seven years. The circumstances of Phillis's life did not permit her to make many black friends, and Tanner is one of the very few that she had.

book would also include letters. The book was never published, but the proposal is evidence that she did continue to write poetry after her marriage. Many of the poems listed in the proposal either appeared under different titles or were lost altogether. In the past, even with the support of the Wheatleys and with her good reputation among prominent whites, she had not been able to get her first book published in Boston. Perhaps it was too much to hope for now with the poor economy and without the help of her white friends.

Early in 1780, some time after John Peters was listed as having paid taxes on the house on Queen Street, the Peters family moved to Wilmington, Massachusetts. Exactly when or why is unknown today. Whether or not Phillis was unhappy there is also not known because, as many have written, she never complained. A prayer she is believed to have written does put into words her fears about childbirth. In the prayer, she asks for God's help to "bring a clean thing out of an/ unclean." It would have been written during her first pregnancy in 1779. Phillis apparently had two more children after she and her husband moved to Wilmington.

Most of the stories of her suffering in Wilmington have come from the biography written by Susannah Wheatley's great-grandniece, Margaretta Matilda Odell, some fifty years after Phillis's death. In *Memoir*, Odell wrote that "Phillis suffered much from privation," and that she faced hardships she was not strong enough to endure. Phillis and her family had returned to Boston by late summer 1784. Margaretta Odell's account does not mention John Peters in the return. According to her, Phillis and her three children were taken in and were cared for by a niece of Mrs. Wheatley's. Odell went on to write that after six weeks John Peters came and took his family to an apartment he had gotten for them. Various sources have reported that it was a shabby apartment in a boardinghouse in a neglected area of Boston, and that he left Phillis and the children there to fend for themselves. It has also been reported that friends found her there, living in extreme poverty, with two children dead and one near death.

In September of that year, another advertisement appeared in Boston area papers for the proposed second book, and again it attracted no publishers. This proposal and three more of her poems were her last publications before she died. She must have been disappointed that she could not get her second book published, especially after the attention she had always received as a poet. Even more tragic were the deaths of her three children.

On December 5, 1784, Phillis Wheatley Peters died. Today the cause and the place of her death are unknown. The notice of her death in the *Massachusetts Independent Chronicle and Universal Advertiser* seems at odds with the popular notion that she died in squalor and utterly alone. In the quaint language of the day, the notice reads: "Last Lord's Day, died Mrs. Phillis Peters (formerly Phillis

Phillis Wheatley's obituary, boxed in red, ran a few days after her death, which occurred on December 5, 1784.

Wheatley) aged 31, known to the literary world by her celebrated miscellaneous Poems. Her funeral is to be this afternoon, at 4 o'clock, from the house lately improved by Mr. Todd, nearly opposite Dr. Bulfinch's, at West-Boston, where her friends and acquaintances are desired to attend."

Phillis's children had all died before her, and it is not clear where her husband was at the time of her passing. According to Odell, none of Phillis's friends knew of her death. Yet someone cared enough to see that a notice was printed in the papers. It is believed that her funeral took place in a house in a very prestigious neighborhood. Although no one knows where she is buried, a grand-niece of Susannah Wheatley's passed Phillis's funeral procession on what was then known as Queen Street. Therefore, one theory is that she is buried in the nearby Old Granary Burial Grounds, along with her third child. Another theory is that Phillis herself is responsible for the anonymity of her gravesite. Because she was devoutly religious, she may have believed that only God should know a true Christian's final resting place.

This is a photograph of the Old Granary Burial Grounds in Boston, Massachusetts, where Phillis Wheatley is rumored to have been buried. Founded in 1660, this cemetery sits on the former site of the town's grain storage area. For this reason, it was named Old Granary.

7. Let My People Go

In *Memoir*, Margaretta Odell expressed her fear that Phillis Wheatley would not be remembered. Nothing could be farther from reality. Immediately following her death, a poem titled "Elegy on the Death of a Late/Celebrated Poetess" appeared in *The Boston Magazine*. Written by someone known only as Horatio, it was a fitting tribute to one who had composed so many elegies herself in remembrance of others. Also a fitting tribute was that Phillis's first book of poems was finally reprinted in America two years after she died.

For a long time, Odell's 1834 biography of the poet was considered the most authoritative. She wrote it to do more than simply tell about Phillis's experiences. Researching and sharing the details of Phillis's life was Odell's way of showing that all the reasons given to justify slavery of blacks and oppression of women were wrong. She was anxious to make people understand that Phillis Wheatley was not "a solitary instance of African genius." In other words, what Phillis had done, other Africans would also be able to do when given the same

What credulous beauties his art
 had undone ;
He swore that his faith should invio-

That his heart and those fair ones were
 victims to me ;
I told him those victims and faith I
 despise,
And from such examples would learn
 to be wise,
That I would never prostitute virtue

Or smell at a rose, to be hurt by a
 thorn.

Was the perjur'd betrayer asham'd
 of his guilt,
Was his passion on virtue, not wan-
 tonly built,
Was his breast as sincere, as his oaths
 were profane,
I could fancy (I own I could fancy)
 the swain ;
But experience has taught me 'tis
 dang'rous to trust,
And folly to think the canoyer be just ;
So I'll stifle my flame, and reject him
 with scorn,
Least I grasp at the rose and be hurt
 by the thorn.

The Answer.

TO judge of him now, by what he
 has been,
To years of discretion from that of
 sixteen;
What beauties he followed, what women betray'd,
(Aware of their wiles, of marriage
 afraid)
Would injure yourself, call in question his sense,
Make doubtful your merit, your
 virtue pretence ;
Then believe him in earnest, away
 with your scorn,
Receive but the rose, you'll be safe
 from the thorn.

For the BOSTON MAGAZINE.

Elegy on the Death of a late celebrated Poetess.

IF conscious sense of genius yet remains;
Of lofty verse, and soft poetic strains

shall not the muse a grateful tribute
 rear.
And drop the silent, sympathetic

If aught that glows within the friend-
 ly breast,
That weeps at tales of woe, or hearts
 opprest ;
With me your sympathizing tribute
 pay,
And to her peaceful manes inscribe

Ye ! who her talents and her virtues knew,
With grief's spontaneous tears her
 urn bedew.
She too comply'd with nature's sacred tye,
She gently wip'd the sorrow-stream-
 ing eye,
As if by heaven inspir'd, did she re-
 late,
The souls grand entrance at the sacred gate ! *
And shall the honour, which she oft
 apply'd,
To other's reliques, be to hers deny'd ?
 O that the muse, dear spirit ! own'd
 thy art,
To soften grief and captivate the
 heart,
Then should these lines in numbers
 soft array'd,
Preserve thy mem'ry from oblivion's
 shade ;
But O ! how vain the wish that
 friendship pays,
Since her own volumes are her great-
 est praise.

 As Orpheus play'd the list'ning
 herds among,
They own'd the magic of his powerful song ;
Mankind no more their savage nature kept,
And foes to music, wonder'd how
 they wept.
So PHILLIS tun'd her sweet melli-
 fluous lyre ;
(Harmonious numbers bid the soul
 aspire)
While Afric's untaught race with
 transport heard,
 They

* Page 488 of this vol.

A poem by Horatio titled "Elegy on the Death of a Late/Celebrated Poetess" was published in *The Boston Magazine* immediately after Phillis's death. Part of the poem is boxed in blue.

Major Martin R. Delaney, shown here in a portrait from 1860, was an author, a freemason, and a well-known abolitionist. He often referred to Phillis Wheatley in his writings about the rights to freedom and to equality for African Americans.

chance. In *Memoir*, Odell appealed to those she called "Friends of liberty" to end the oppression and ill treatment of black people. Using Phillis as an example, Odell made the point that women were fit for more than domestic work.

Odell was not alone in using Phillis Wheatley in the name of abolition to show that black people were human and capable of learning. Others, black and white, would also point to the black poet from western Africa to further their cause. After all, Phillis had an international reputation from having published her book in England, and her fame could be helpful in furthering the cause of abolition. She was useful because she not only could read and write, but she wrote poetry, something long considered proof of great intelligence. Benjamin Rush, a white physician and an abolitionist writing in 1773, called her a genius and praised her accomplishments. Phillis's brilliance was also referred to by Martin R. Delaney, a well-educated free black man who wrote books and essays on civil rights after her death. He made specific references to Phillis in his abolitionist writings to show that blacks were not inferior. Phillis's example proved valuable in the abolitionist cause. Unfortunately, the interest in her slave status and race overshadowed the interest in her poetry for many years.

Little had changed, then, since the letter "To the Publick" attached to her first book announced the poems of "PHILLIS, a young Negro Girl, who was but a few Years since, brought an uncultivated Barbarian from Africa." The words in the letter were not meant to be unkind. Their point was to show how far she had been brought and how much could be accomplished through Christian teachings. However, the term "barbarian," even when used by well-meaning people, was horribly offensive. Phillis bore such insensitive treatment well, though, and sometimes made references to her race herself. Yet when Phillis spoke of herself as an African, it may have been her own quiet way of reminding everyone, as the abolitionists did, of what an African and a slave was capable. Her accomplishments disproved the prejudiced notion that blacks were inferior to whites. She did not try to hide her African roots from her readers. She did not appear to be ashamed of her people. She did not believe, as some have said, that blacks had done anything to deserve their condition. In her poem "On the Death of General Wooster," she refers to her race as "blameless."

Yet both then and later, she would be criticized for staying in her "place" as a slave, even though she had many privileges that other enslaved people did not have. A common belief among later black writers, scholars, and activists was that, because of those privileges, she was not concerned about the problems of black people in her time, especially concerning the issue of slavery. This is not so. Perhaps Phillis wished to write more often about freedom for all humankind than just for any one group of people. However, even in such poems, she sometimes quietly slipped in a line or two showing her concern for her fellow Africans. A good example is her poem "To The Right Honourable William, Earl of Dartmouth, His Majesty's Principal Secretary of State for North America," in which Phillis wrote: "No more, of grievance unredress'd complain; Or injur'd Rights, or groan beneath the chain, Which Wanton Tyranny, with lawless hand, Made to enslave." These lines indicate her desire for an end to slavery. Phillis was also aware of her own particular condition, that she had been stolen from her home, causing her parents much unhappiness.

Phillis's belief in Christian teachings would not allow her to dwell only on herself. Therefore she also

These lines from Phillis Wheatley's poem, written when she was about nineteen years old, show how fervently she opposed slavery. The poem describes her own particular situation of having been kidnapped from Africa and portrays the kidnapper as someone without pity. She emphasizes the cruelty of the act that caused her parents such pain:

I, young in life by seeming cruel fate
Was snatch'd from Afric's fancy'd happy seat;
What pangs excruciating must molest,
What sorrows labour in my parents breast?
Steel'd was that soul and by no misery mov'd
That from a father seiz'd his babe belov'd;
Such, such my case. And can I then but pray
Others may never feel tyrannic sway?

—Phillis Wheatley
from "To the Right Honourable William, Earl of Dartmouth, His Majesty's Principal Secretary of State for North America, & c."

included others in this poem about freedom, praying that they would never feel the tyranny that she and her African family had suffered.

The Christian principles that Phillis had been taught from the moment she entered the Wheatley home as an eight-year-old child were always part of the solution to any of her problems. She was deeply religious and felt that the concerns of slaves and of Christians went hand in hand. She wrote as much to Reverend Samson Occum in a letter dated February 11, 1774. Reverend Samson Occum was a Mohegan Native American who converted to Christianity and became a Presbyterian minister. Phillis had met him in the home of the Wheatleys as their friend, which explains why the two of them would correspond with each other. Another reason they corresponded is that they shared similar concerns. Both were from groups that had, in one way or another, been separated from their homelands and had suffered oppression.

Phillis's letter to Occum has come to be recognized as a strong antislavery statement. It outlined her firm belief that God created all people to love freedom and stated that, as far as she was concerned, religious liberty and liberty in one's everyday life were inseparable. In the letter, she spoke out against those who said one thing but did another, referring to the colonists who said that all men should be free, but who still kept blacks enslaved. She echoed these same beliefs in the poem she wrote on the occasion of Major General David Wooster's death.

Both the poem and the letter to Occum show that she was aware of her duty as a member of an oppressed people, even if others did not always think so.

Indeed, after her death, some black critics called her insulting names such as the Boston Aunt Jemima and a female Uncle Tom. Both Aunt Jemima and Uncle Tom are uncomplimentary names for blacks who are said to take more interest in whites and their well-being than they take in themselves and their own people. This interest can be accompanied by extremely servile behavior. Such name-calling against Phillis was unfair. It showed that the individuals doing it had read very little of her poetry, and had read it without truly grasping its meaning.

Uncle Tom images, showing an overly obedient black man such as in this A. S. Seer drawing from the 1880s, added to antislavery feelings in the North.

More understanding critics of Phillis Wheatley have put her writings in the context of the historical times in which she lived and wrote. For instance, they have tried to show how her writing and thinking were influenced by religious issues of the day, by the wars that were going on all around her, and by patriotism and politics. How could she help but write about the American Revolution? She was an eyewitness to much of it. British troops paraded right past the Wheatley home on King Street. The Boston Massacre occurred within walking distance of the house. Various meeting houses used for planning attacks and other strategies were located a block or two away. The poetry that Phillis wrote about these matters expresses her hope that independence for the colonists meant independence for all.

Her name-callers apparently did not understand how much freedom meant to her. However, William H. Robinson, the literary historian who wrote extensively about Phillis Wheatley, counted the number of times the words "free" and "freedom" appear in her poetry. In the 451-word poem "Liberty and Peace" alone, the word "freedom" appears four times, along with words that mean the same or nearly the same thing, such as "liberty" and "independent," each of which appears once. There is no doubt that freedom and independence were foremost in Phillis's thoughts. Because she met and corresponded with so many famous people, such as Benjamin Franklin and George Washington, and because she visited the homes of very important Bostonians, perhaps it was easy for some critics to forget that she was a slave. Yet she was never allowed to forget it, not even after she was freed.

8. From Slavery to Freedom?

It is a great wonder that Phillis Wheatley ever wrote a line of poetry. She had lived such a strange life, having been kidnapped as a child and been taken so far from her home and her country. Did she have brothers and sisters? Did she play games? What were her parents like? What was her African name? These are questions that probably will never be answered.

Phillis wrote in one of her poems that mercy brought her from Africa, but was it mercy? Some say she was lucky that she fell into the hands of the Wheatleys, lucky that she was a slave in New England instead of in the South. How could anyone be lucky to be a slave? Wouldn't she have been even luckier if she had never been a slave at all? When the Wheatleys freed Phillis, she must have been very happy. Yet she must have also wondered what she was to do after so many years of slavery, especially because she had been treated so well. Her skills included reading and writing, and it seems logical that she would have been taught to cook and to sew, as were most women. According to Odell in *Memoir*, after Phillis was

This engraving of a seamstress at her sewing machine was created in 1807. It is believed that Phillis Wheatley worked as a seamstress after her release from slavery.

freed, her time "was chiefly occupied with her books, her pen, and her needle." She is also reported, by at least one account, to have worked as a seamstress following her release from slavery. Still, she must have been concerned about what would become of her after Susannah Wheatley died. After the deaths of John and Mary Wheatley, there were no more Wheatleys Phillis could turn to for help. Nathaniel was still living in England, and there is no record of further contact between him and Phillis. He died in 1783, the year before Phillis died.

It was difficult for any woman to live on her own during those days. Marriage must have seemed the only option open to her. However, most accounts of her marriage indicate that it was not a happy one. Most accounts of her husband, John Peters, say that it was his fault their marriage was not happy. Even her friend Obour Tanner wrote that "poor Phillis let herself down by marrying," which seems to suggest that there was some truth to the reports. Odell also recorded that after John Peters removed Phillis and the children from the home of Susannah Wheatley's niece, where they had lived for six weeks, he took them to a "mean" boarding-house. In other words, it was rundown. He left them there. Some say he was taken to debtor's prison, a jail for people who could not pay their bills. When debating

This debtor's prison in Accomack County, Virginia, was built around 1785. Until the late eighteenth century, debtors, or people who could not pay their bills, were often imprisoned in such a building. Sometimes nonviolent criminals were also housed in debtor's prisons.

whether their poverty was his fault, it must be remembered that they lived in a slaveholding society and that free blacks were subjected to much of the same treatment as were slaves. John Peters's difficulty in obtaining work to support his family may have had something to do with his being black in a racially prejudiced society.

Wherever John Peters was and whatever causes led him there, apparently Phillis was left to the task of supporting herself and her children by working outside the home. It was not unusual for colonial women to sell their services outside the home, though their work did not pay very much. Women did laundry, scrubbed, baked, sewed, and performed other kinds of domestic duties. Ironically, these were the very jobs that Phillis seldom, if ever, had to do while she was a slave. She had always been sickly, and once she was no longer living with the Wheatleys and had to survive on little money, she might also have been undernourished. This means that she might not have had enough wholesome food to keep her healthy and strong. Her infant children might have been undernourished, too, and that might be why they died so young. If the place where they lived was unclean, as was reported in Odell's *Memoir*, then disease seems another likely cause of their illness and their death.

As for the charge that Phillis wrote poems on the deaths of other children but none on her own, one can imagine that it was too painful for a mother to write about the deaths of her own beloved children. It seems that she did not write any poems on the deaths of Susannah, John, Mary, or Nathaniel Wheatley either, which might be an indication that she simply could not write about death when the departed were so close to her. She also might have thought it was improper, as William H. Robinson has speculated, "to write of her personal situation publicly." It is too bad that she was not still writing to Obour Tanner during her last years. So many questions might now have answers. What were her children's names? Were they boys or girls? How did Phillis really feel about their father, John Peters? She might have felt more comfortable discussing her personal life with the woman she called "dear friend" and "sister." Obour Tanner lived until June 21, 1835.

When the friends whom Odell mentioned in *Memoir* found Phillis at the boardinghouse, she was reportedly very sick herself and her third child was described as "sick unto death," which probably meant the child was dying. Had Phillis risen up from slavery or had she sunk to a level below it? One can't help but remember that once, when she was ill in the Wheatley home, the doctors prescribed sea air for her asthma, and she was sent to Britain. It is ironic that her life as a slave seems to have been better than it was as a free woman.

If, after the Wheatleys' deaths, Phillis's situation really became as bad as has been described, then she would have needed to make money with her poems. Her thoughts must have turned once again to writing the kinds of poems that would be of interest to Bostonians. In fact, the last three poems she published in the year she died are such poems, two of her typical elegies and a poem on peace: "An Elegy to Dr. Samuel Cooper," "Liberty and Peace," and "To Mr. and Mrs. ___, On the Death of Their Infant Son." As before, she planned to dedicate the book of poems she advertised to an important person, this time Benjamin Franklin, probably with the hope that dedicating it to him would help to get it published. Unfortunately Phillis did not live to see the book published. She died on December 5, 1784, at age thirty-one, in the country to which she had been brought by force, but in which she had remained by choice.

9. Legacy: Her Truth Goes Marching On

Today, at the dawn of the twenty-first century, writers, scholars, and teachers recognize Phillis Wheatley as a pioneering literary figure and an enthusiastic supporter of antislavery. Much is made of the fact that she was the first African American to publish a book of poems. Just as amazing and noteworthy is the fact that she was only the second American woman of any race to publish a book of poems. Anne Bradstreet was the first. One might say that more than two centuries after Phillis's death, she is still achieving her freedom. It is certain that she is still being discovered. Few, if any, poets write couplets anymore. However, today's poets, especially women, see Phillis as an inspiration. Her voice began to be heard through her poetry and her letters at a time when enslaved black people were literally being muzzled, and she is now recognized for her courage.

Since the reprinting of her book in America for the first time in 1786, it has been reprinted dozens of times in both America and Europe. The scholar William H. Robinson has noted the many countries in which the name and the poetry of Phillis Wheatley have become known since the first small volume was published in England. Her views have also become known through the publication of her letters almost a century after her death, and through an even later volume of her poems and letters. The publication of her letters, written to famous people, such as then-general George Washington, the countess of Huntingdon, and the earl of Dartmouth, is important not only for the information the letters provide about Phillis Wheatley but also as a measure of the high regard scholars had for her work. One might say that these publications are also important because they represent widespread interest in her work.

At one time, it was difficult to find anyone who made an effort to interpret, evaluate, and enjoy her poetry without being overly interested in or influenced by her African roots. A literary historian named Benjamin Brawley was one of the earliest twentieth-century scholars to take a different approach to studying her poetry. He attempted to make the readers of his day understand that although Alexander Pope, the eighteenth-century English poet Wheatley admired, might have been a model for her work, so too were the "greater Latin authors," who were also Pope's models, and whom she also had studied. As did other poets, Wheatley followed the literary trends of her day. She had no African models.

Since Brawley's earlier efforts, dozens of books and articles have been written about Phillis Wheatley, and a

Benjamin Brawley (1882-1939) was a prominent African American author and educator. *Women of Achievement* (c. 1919) is one of Brawley's numerous books and articles on African American culture.

variety of adjectives have been added to the racial ones used to describe her. Words such as "legendary," to denote that her fame continues, and "revolutionary," which signals a completely new understanding of her and her poetry, have been used in recent years. An autographed copy of Phillis Wheatley's 1773 book of poems sells for more than $20,000 today. Schools, other buildings, and a variety of organizations have been named in her honor, and scholarships have been funded in her name. Phillis Wheatley festivals and conferences have been organized and attended by many well-known poets and scholars. One of the most elegant tributes to her to this date has been written by the poet June Jordan, who called her Phillis Miracle because she endured so much and yet still wrote poetry.

According to Robinson, Phillis wrote more than 100 poems, published in a variety of newspapers and magazines, all in her short lifetime. After Phillis died, John Peters advertised in the paper for the return of manuscripts of her unpublished poems. Supposedly they were returned to him, but they were never published. When he vanished, they vanished with him.

In 1998, though, a poem written by Phillis Wheatley titled "Ocean" was discovered in someone's attic, and it was sold at auction for nearly $70,000. As a child, Phillis had been sold to the Wheatleys for a few shillings, and today a single poem of hers is worth thousands of dollars!

"Ocean" is believed to have been written shortly after her return voyage from Britain in 1773, and it was listed in the 1779 proposal advertised in Boston newspapers when she was trying to publish her second book of poems. The original handwritten manuscript of the poem was recently on display for a time in the Newseum, a museum of news located in Arlington, Virginia. At an event organized at the Newseum on February 4, 1999, Rita Dove offered a dramatic reading of Wheatley's poem. Dove is a well-known poet and was formerly America's poet laureate, meaning she was honored for her artistic excellence as one of the nation's finest poets. It is fitting that an event was also held at

Phillis Wheatley wrote "Ocean," a seventy-line ode to the sea, in 1773. An ode is a serious poem that often expresses strong personal emotions on a particular subject. "Ocean" was part of a collection that was to be published as Wheatley's second book. Unfortunately, the collection of poems was lost before it ever got published. "Ocean" did not appear in Wheatley's first book, Poems on Various Subjects, Religious and Moral.

More than two hundred years would pass before the only known copy of "Ocean" surfaced in someone's attic. The value of the poem was understood by Mark E. Mitchell, the historian and rare documents dealer who paid nearly $70,000 for the yellowing and creased manuscript.

Since Mitchell bought the poem at an auction, it has been made available to readers in several publications. "Ocean" was printed in the Washington Post on February 11, 1999. "Ocean" also appeared in the Journal of Early American History and in a volume entitled Phillis Wheatley and the Origins of African American Literature.

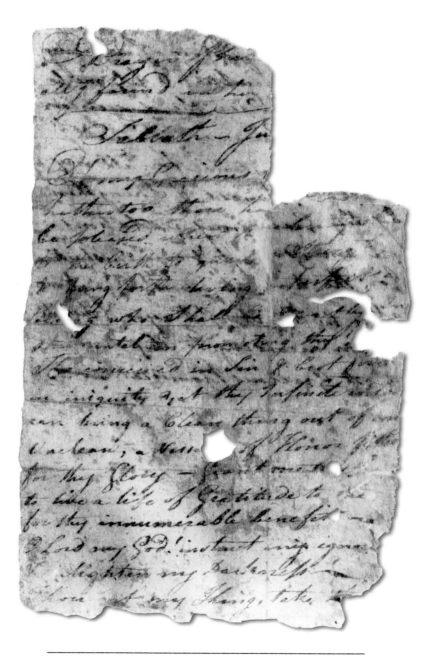

This handwritten prayer by Phillis Wheatley
was found in her Bible on June 13, 1779.

the Old South Church, where Phillis was baptized, to celebrate the recovery of the poem.

It is interesting that a 1999 news release on the Mitchell Archives Web site announcing the rediscovery of Phillis Wheatley refers to her as a black poet, rather than simply a poet. Phillis may always be something of a curiosity, because she was the first of her kind. However, scholars such as William H. Robinson and poets such as June Jordan, among many others, have enabled the world to see that Phillis Wheatley had many sides. They have enabled others to see that she was a gifted poet, not just a slave or a woman.

June Jordan called her Phillis Miracle, and she was a miracle. Against the odds, she survived the Middle Passage. Against the odds, she became a poet. Finally, she has taken her rightful place at the head of an African American literary tradition. Recent scholars have written that "no single writer has contributed more to the founding of African American literature." The inclusion of Phillis Wheatley's poetry in almost all the important books about American literature indicates that she is beginning to be recognized for her pioneering efforts as an American writer. When several people, whom she admired and trusted, urged her to go back to Africa as a missionary, she chose to stay in America. After all she had lived through, she knew she had a right to consider America her home.

Timeline

1753   Phillis Wheatley is believed to have been born in the Senegambia region of western Africa.

1761   Wheatley arrives in Boston, Massachusetts, aboard the slave ship *Phillis*. She is purchased by John Wheatley.

1767   Phillis Wheatley's poem "On Messrs. Hussey and Coffin" is published. It is her first publication.

1769   Wheatley's poem on Joseph Sewall's death is published.

1770   Wheatley writes her poem "On the Death of Mr. Snider Murder'd by Richardson."

Wheatley is believed to have written "On the Affray in King-Street" not long after the Boston Massacre takes place.

"On the Death of the Rev. George

Whitefield. 1770," published October 2, begins Wheatley's reputation as a poet.

1771   On August 18, Wheatley is baptized by Reverend Samuel Cooper and becomes a member of Boston's Old South Church.

1772   Wheatley's first proposal for a volume of poems is published in a newspaper.

1773   Wheatley sails for London on May 8 with Nathaniel Wheatley. She returns to Boston in July because of the illness of Susannah Wheatley.

Phillis Wheatley's *Poems on Various Subjects, Religious and Moral* is published in September in London.

In a letter dated October 18, Wheatley tells David Wooster that she has been freed by the Wheatleys.

The Boston Tea Party occurs on December 16. Samuel Adams and about fifty other colonists dump containers of tea into Boston Harbor.

1774   Susannah Wheatley dies on March 3.

1778   John Wheatley dies on March 12.

Wheatley marries John Peters on April 1.

Mary Wheatley Lathrop dies in September.

1779   Wheatley's final proposal for another book of poems, which was to include letters, is published in the newspaper. Most of the poems and letters are lost in later years, and the book is never published.

1783   Nathaniel Wheatley dies in Britain.

1784   Phillis Wheatley dies on December 5.

1786   The first American printing of Wheatley's book takes place.

1998   Wheatley's poem "Ocean" is discovered in an attic and is sold for nearly $70,000.

Glossary

abolition (a-buh-LIH-shun) The official ending of the practice of slavery.

affray (uh-FRAY) A fight in a public place.

anonymity (a-nuh-NIH-muh-tee) The state of not being known.

auction (AWK-shun) A sale of property at which buyers bid against each other for the individual items.

baptize (BAP-tyz) To sprinkle or to immerse someone in water to show that person's acceptance into the Christian faith.

bondage (BAHN-dihj) Slavery; ownership of a person by another person.

boycott (BOY-kaht) An organized effort to refrain from buying goods and services from a company to gain a result or change the company's practices.

broadside (BRAWD-syd) A large sheet of paper that is printed on one side.

colony (KAH-luh-nee) A large group of people who have left their own country to live in a new land but are still ruled by the leaders and the laws of their old country.

decorum (dih-KOR-um) Correct, socially acceptable behavior.

degraded (dih-GRAYD-ed) Suffering a loss of reputation; made lower.

diabolic (dy-uh-BAH-lihk) Evil.

domestic (duh-MEHS-tik) Relating to or used within a household.

elite (ay-LEET) A small group of people in a larger group who have more power, privileges, or wealth than the rest of the group.

excerpts (EK-surpts) Sections or passages taken from a larger document.

excruciating (ek-SKROO-shee-ayt-ing) Very painful.

exported (EK-sport-ed) A product sold and transported to another country.

frontispiece (FRUN-tuh-spees) A picture at the beginning of a book, usually facing the title page.

guineas (GIH-neez) Old units of British money that were used between 1663 and 1813.

headnote (HEHD-noht) A brief note at the top of a page that explains or comments on what follows.

hypocrisy (hih-PAH-kruh-see) Pretending to have high principles, beliefs, or feelings.

import (IM-port) To bring in from another country.

insurrection (in-suh-REK-shun) Rebelling against someone's control, usually with weapons.

lamenting (luh-MENT-ing) Feeling or expressing sorrow.

martyr (MAR-ter) Someone who dies or is killed for a cause or a principle.

menial (MEE-nee-uhl) Requiring little or no skill.

missionary (MIH-shuh-ner-ee) Someone sent by a church to another country to spread religion or to do medical work.

molest (muh-LEST) To bother or to disturb a person.

muse (MYOOZ) Someone or something that inspires a poet; a gifted poet.

pagan (PAY-gun) One who follows an unpopular religion or no religion.

parliament (PAR-lih-mint) The lawmakers of a country.

patriarchy (PAY-tree-ar-kee) A society in which men have the power and the control.

patronage (PAY-truh-nihj) To help someone through encouragement or monetary support.

polygamy (puh-LIH-guh-mee) The practice of having many spouses, especially wives, at one time.

primer (PRIH-mur) A book used to teach young children to read.

privation (pry-VAY-shun) Lacking in necessities.

procured (pruh-KYURD) Tried to obtain something.

redemption (rih-DEHM-shun) Saving or improving something. In Christianity, saved from sin by Christ's death.

reproached (rih-PROHCHT) Blamed.

robust (roh-BUHST) Strong and healthy.

sable (SAY-buhl) Very dark.

servile (SUR-vuhl) Too obedient; too willing to do whatever someone else wants.

squalor (SKWAH-lur) Shabbiness and dirtiness caused by poverty.

symmetry (SIH-muh-tree) Harmony or beauty of form that results from perfectly balanced proportions.

tyranny (TEER-uh-nee) Cruel use of power over others.

Additional Resources

To learn more about Phillis Wheatley, check out these books and Web sites:

Books

Greene, Carol. *Phillis Wheatley: First African-American Poet*. Chicago: Children's Press, 1995.

Gregson, Susan R. *Phillis Wheatley*. Mankato, Minnesota: Bridgestone Books, 2002.

Rinaldi, Ann. *Hang a Thousand Trees with Ribbons: The Story of Phillis Wheatley*. San Diego, California: Gulliver Books, 1996.

Salisbury, Cynthia. *Phillis Wheatley: Legendary African-American Poet*. Berkeley Heights, New Jersey: Enslow Publishers, 2001.

Sherrow, Victoria. *Phillis Wheatley*. New York: Chelsea Juniors, 1992.

Web Sites

Due to the changing nature of Internet links, PowerPlus Books has developed an online list of Web sites related to the subject of this book. This site is updated regularly. Please use this link to access the list:

www.powerkidslinks.com/lalt/wheatley/

Bibliography

Franklin, John Hope and Alfred A. Moss Jr. *From Slavery to Freedom: A History of African Americans, Seventh Edition*. New York: McGraw-Hill, Inc., 1994.

Iliffe, John. *Africans: The History of a Continent*. Cambridge, United Kingdom: Cambridge University Press, 1995.

Lewis, Earl and Robin D. G. Kelley. *To Make Our World Anew: A History of African Americans*. New York: Oxford University Press, 2000.

Mason Jr., Julian D., ed. *The Poems of Phillis Wheatley, Revised and Enlarged Edition*. Chapel Hill, North Carolina: The University of North Carolina Press, 1989.

Robinson, William Henry. *Phillis Wheatley and Her Writings*. New York: Garland Press, 1984.

————. *Black American Beginnings*. Detroit: The Broadside Press, 1975.

Watkins, Richard, author and illustrator. *Slavery: Bondage Throughout History*. Boston: Houghton Mifflin Company, 2001.

Index

About the Author

Dr. Jacquelyn Y. McLendon is an associate professor of English and the director of black studies at the College of William and Mary in Virginia. Her book, titled *The Politics of Color in the Fiction of Jessie Fauset and Nella Larsen*, focuses on two black women writers of the Harlem Renaissance. She has written several articles and numerous literary encyclopedia entries on writers such as Langston Hughes, Gwendolyn Brooks, and Alice Walker. She is working on a book about the Harlem Renaissance that will include visual artists and performers of that era.

Credits

Photo Credits

Cover: North Wind Picture Archives (portrait); courtesy of the Massachusetts Historical Society (background), pp. 14, 28, 85 Prints and Photographs Division, Library of Congress; pp. 4, 9, 20, 40 North Wind Picture Archives; p. 6 courtesy of the Library Company of Philadelphia; p. 8 courtesy of Map Division, The New York Public Library, Astor, Lenox and Tilden Foundations; pp. 10, 11, 59 (inset) © CORBIS; p. 12 © Underwood & Underwood/CORBIS; pp. 17, 26, 37, 76 courtesy of the Rare Books & Manuscripts Collection, The New York Public Library, Astor, Lenox and Tilden Foundations; pp. 19, 24, 70 Library of Congress Geography and Map Division; p. 22 "photo by Richard Beatty, copyright reserved" 1971; p. 23 © Werner Forman/CORBIS; pp. 30, 36, 51, 59 © Bettmann/CORBIS; p. 34 Coram Foundation, Foundling Museum, London, UK/Bridgeman Art Library; p. 35 © Scala/Art Resource, NY; p. 39 Bridgeman Art Library; p. 42 by courtesy of the National Portrait Gallery, London; pp. 44–45, 61 courtesy of the Massachusetts Historical Society; pp. 46, 80, 95, 98 Photographs and Prints Division, Schomburg Center for Research in Black Culture, The New York Public Library; p. 47 Prints George; p. 49 courtesy, the Detroit Institute of Arts; p. 50 Independence National Historic Park; p. 55 © National Gallery Collection; by kind permission of the Trustees of the National Gallery, London/CORBIS; p. 62 courtesy, Winterthur Museum; p. 64 Library of Congress, Manuscript Division; p. 65 National Gallery of Art, Washington, gift of Edgar William and Bernice Chrysler Garbisch; p. 66 John Murray, 4th Earl of Dunmore by Sir Joshua Reynolds, *Scottish National Portrait Gallery*; p. 68 Emmett Collection, Miriam and Ira D. Wallach Division of Art, Prints, and Photographs; p. 73 Library of Congress, Rare Book and Special Collections Division; p. 77 © Robert Holmes/CORBIS; p. 88 Dover Pictorial Archive Series; p. 89 Library of Congress, Prints and Photographs Division, Historic American Buildings Survey or Historic American Engineering Record, HABS, VA,1-AC,4-1; p. 98 Manuscripts, Archives & Rare Books Division, Schomburg Center For Research in Black Culture.

Editor Leslie Kaplan

Series Design Laura Murawski

Layout Design Corinne Jacob

Photo Researcher Jeffrey Wendt